Isle of Skye

40 Coast and Country Walks

The author and publisher have made every effort to ensure that the information in this publication is accurate, and accept no responsibility whatsoever for any loss, injury or inconvenience experienced by any person or persons whilst using this book.

With thanks to Donald Kennedy, Skye and Lochalsh Access Officer, Highland Council

published by
pocket mountains ltd
6 Church Wynd, Bo'ness EH51 0AN
pocketmountains.com

ISBN-13: 978-0-9554548-8-2

Printed in Poland

Introduction

Skye has long been a mecca for hardy hillwalkers and climbers attracted by the alpine peaks of the Cuillin, the most challenging mountains in Britain. However, the dramatic coastline of the island – also often claimed to be the country's finest – is scarcely less impressive and Skye has scores of varied walks at all levels. This guide contains 40 moderate routes covering all parts of Skye together with the neighbouring island of Raasay. They are intended to give a taste of every aspect of this celebrated landscape and to seek out some of the less visited gems as well as the popular highlights.

Skye is the second largest of the Hebrides and its size often takes visitors by surprise. It covers over 1600 square kilometres and even this figure is misleading due to the island's complex shape, divided into many peninsulas which can make touring the island a major undertaking. This shape gives the island its Gaelic name of An t-Eilean Sgitheanach, meaning the winged isle.

The routes in the book are divided into five areas, each of which is introduced by a summary giving a flavour of its characteristics and a map to locate the starts of the walks.

Safety
Although the routes are termed moderate, much of Skye is a very wild landscape and few of the walks are on waymarked footpaths. Most can be wet underfoot, so good boots are needed. The sketch map accompanying each route is intended to help plan the outing rather than as a navigational aid; the relevant OS or Harvey map should always be taken.

Whilst Skye benefits from the warming effects of the Gulf Stream and is mild in winter, the Stream also brings very rapid changes in the weather. Particularly in spring, it is quite possible to get bright sunshine, sleet, strong wind and rain all within an hour. It is, therefore, advisable to pack wind- and water-proof clothing and adequate warm layers to allow the walks to be enjoyed whatever the weather. Many of the routes would be suitable for families with children in good conditions, although care should be taken on the coastal walks as many of the cliffs are very high and unfenced. Loch Cuithir and the Broadford Marble Line could be done pushing an all-terrain buggy and parts of other walks would also be suitable.

Access and dogs
An effort has been made to include walks which can be done by public transport. However, the lack of buses to some remoter areas and the scheduling that mainly fits around the school day does not make this possible on many walks. The book indicates where public transport can be taken. Further information on timetables can be found at tourist information centres and from Traveline Scotland.

The Land Reform (Scotland) Act in 2003 gave walkers rights of access over most of Scotland away from residential buildings, but with these rights come responsibilities. Remember that much of Skye is a crofting landscape and sheep and cattle-rearing is a difficult business. Always follow the Scottish Outdoor Access Code, and particularly keep dogs on leads during the spring and early summer, steering them well away from both sheep and lambs.

Wildlife

Skye and Raasay are wild landscapes and there is a huge amount to uncover here for the keen birdwatcher or wildlife enthusiast. The coasts of Skye and Raasay are particularly good places to spot otters with a thriving population, whilst both grey and common seals are a common sight. Minke whales and other marine mammals are frequently sighted in the summer months from headlands such as Neist Point, Waternish Point and Rubha Hunish.

In recent years the magnificent white-tailed or sea eagle – Britain's largest bird of prey – has re-established itself across the island. It can be seen almost anywhere, but we would recommend Inver Bay on Raasay for a good chance. Golden eagles, too, have a strong population, particularly around the Cuillin and the Trotternish Ridge. Seabirds such as shags, guillemots and visiting gannets abound around the coastline: Rubha Hunish and An Aird are fabulous places to see breeding razorbills in the spring. Rubha Ardnish overlooking Broadford Bay is very popular with birdwatchers, with a huge range of species being reported.

History

Skye has a rich and bloody history, and many of the walks take in historical sites, from the remains of Iron Age forts to villages deserted during the Clearances and the industrial archaeology of the diatomite works and marble mines.

The mesolithic site at An Corran is one of the oldest in Scotland, dating to the seventh millennium BC, but the earliest remains obvious to walkers are the Bronze Age chambered cairns which were usually associated with burials – there is a good example on the Dun Ringill route. Iron Age sites are much more plentiful in all parts of the island, with the most impressive structures being the brochs. These were circular towers with passageways and staircases within the twin walls enclosing an open area in the centre. There are two brochs near Glenelg on the mainland adjacent to Skye that are well worth seeking out, but there are many other examples on Skye, the finest being on the Waternish Point route. Equally fascinating from this period are the souterrains – underground passages which may have been used for storage. A wonderfully preserved souterrain can be seen at Kilmuir in Trotternish.

Moving into medieval times, Skye was dominated by two great clans, the MacLeods and the MacDonalds, frequently at war with one another. This period was one of great bloodshed, from the battle at Coire na Creiche by the Fairy Pools to the massacre at Trumpan Church on the Waternish Point walk. This period gave rise to the many ruined castles scattered all over the island, from Hugh's Castle and Duntulm in Trotternish to Dun Scaith Castle and Knock in Sleat.

The Jacobite uprising led by Prince Charles Edward Stuart was utterly defeated at Culloden near Inverness in 1746 and began a more recent dark time for the islanders. First was the romantic story of the flight of 'Bonnie Prince Charlie' through the island, aided by Flora MacDonald, his original escape to Skye from Uist being made famous throughout the world by the *Skye Boat Song*. Charles spent five days on Skye before his flight took him to the mainland and eventually back to France, but Prince Charlie's Cave where he spent his last night is visited on one walk.

In the aftermath of Culloden the Highlanders were ruthlessly repressed, with tartan and written Gaelic (even the bible) banned, together with the bearing of arms. The clan system collapsed as the chiefs turned their back on their people and became mere landlords. What followed were the notorious Clearances. People were forced onto the least fertile parts of the land to make way for sheep, their homes burnt down to prevent their return. Many sought a new life across the Atlantic, and songs, dances and placenames from Skye have made their way around the world. Ruined houses dating from the time of the clearances can be seen all over Skye and Raasay, those on the Clearance Villages, Hallaig and Screapadal routes being particularly poignant.

Late in the 19th century the crofters began to fight back, with uprisings such as the Battle of the Braes and the Glendale riots bringing their plight to the attention of the nation. New laws were passed to give crofters security of tenure. Attempts were made to set up new industries on the island, from the diatomite of Loch Cuithir to the Raasay ironstone mines. Although these eventually failed, by the late 20th century the fortunes of the island had turned as the population began to increase once more. Today the island's economy is more secure and attempts are being made to revive the Gaelic language which had been in severe decline.

Accommodation
Skye has a huge range of places to stay to suit every purse, from luxury hotels to budget hostels and campsites. Even so, the island is very popular, particularly in July and August when every bed on the island can be full and it becomes essential to book ahead.

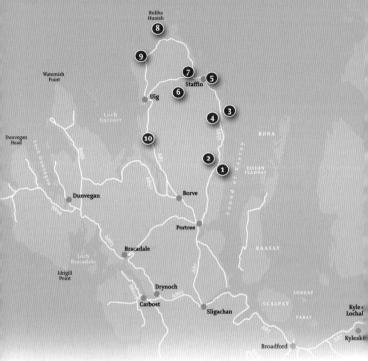

Skye's most northerly peninsula, Trotternish is one of the most spectacular landscapes in Britain. Its backbone is the longest ridge on Skye but its two sides could not be more different. To the west the ridge is a gentle moorland sweeping down to the sea and a coastline of bays and inlets, whilst to the east the ridge collapses abruptly in a great escarpment of broken cliffs with tottering pinnacles below. This is Europe's largest landslip, and it has formed a unique landscape. Most famous are the Old Man of Storr, an

upstanding finger of rock standing guard over a hidden sanctuary, and the Quiraing, a fortress of crazy rock towers. Both have unforgettable views over to the mainland.

The Trotternish coastline may be less celebrated as apart from the Kilt Rock much of its cliffs are hidden from motorists, but the explorer on foot will find it to be a match for the ridge. The walker is free to explore the many secret corners of the coast in peace, with stacks, pinnacles, arches, caves and bays around every corner.

Trotternish

1 **Bearreraig Bay** 8
Watch your step as you climb down a steep path to explore this Site of Special Scientific Interest

2 **The Old Man of Storr** 10
Although it attracts a lot of traffic, this route is a great introduction to the wilder side of the island

3 **Brothers' Point** 12
Follow in the footsteps of the early Christians as you soak up some wonderfully wild coastal views

4 **Lealt and Loch Cuithir** 14
Delve into Skye's less-known industrial heritage beneath the impressive Trotternish Ridge

5 **An Corran – the dinosaur beach** 16
Head for the beach and you will be following in the giant three-toed footsteps of the Hadrosaur

6 **Bioda Buidhe** 18
Avoid the crowds and enjoy the best views on this quieter stretch of the spectacular Trotternish Ridge

7 **The Quiraing** 20
Rocky pinnacles, sudden cliffs and lush green plateaus await in a strange landscape full of surprises

8 **Rubha Hunish** 22
A more challenging walk out to the most northerly point on Skye – don't forget your binoculars!

9 **The Cave of Gold** 24
Look out for dolphins, porpoises and basking sharks as you drift along this entertaining bit of coastline

10 **Hugh's Castle** 26
An easy walk to a tranquil spot with lovely views over Loch Snizort and the Waternish peninsula

Bearreraig Bay

Distance 2km Time 1 hour 30
Terrain very steep path, pebbly shore
Map OS Explorer 408 Access bus (57) from
Portree can be taken to the start of the
road at the far end of the Storr Lochs

Step back in time by descending the
steep path down to Bearreraig Bay, where
dinosaurs roamed 170 million years ago
and their fossil remains are still being
found today. The natural curve of the bay
provides a sheltered spot for fossil
hunting, wildlife watching or sunbathing
on the pebbly shore. This walk can be
combined with an exploration of the
Old Man of Storr just a short way along
the A855.

Start the walk at the end of the minor
road which leaves the A855 from Portree
just after the Storr Lochs and has a
Scottish Hydro Electric sign. Here there is
parking for a small number of cars next to
a cottage and the winding house for a

funicular railway which descends to
the hydro power station far below.
Go through the gate on the right of the
building – it is signed for the beach – and
turn left immediately beyond. The other
sign pointing right here is the start of a
strenuous, pathless trek to Portree.
The path ends at a viewpoint with
interpretative panels and an outlook
across the beach; on a calm day it is
sometimes possible to spot dolphins or
porpoises from here as they pass through
the sound between Skye and the offshore
islands of Rona and Raasay.

Follow the small path starting on the
right which falls away so steeply that it
can look daunting. However, while the
descent is steep and can be slippery after
rain, the path is well used and has
constructed steps and a handrail where it
comes close to the edge of the cliff.
Follow the zigzags down towards the bay,
coming close to the funicular railway

◂ The cliffs at Bearreraig Bay

further down. The railway services the power station, where electricity is generated by water diverted from the Storr Lochs through two huge metal pipes to drive the turbines. The power station, which opened in 1952, generated the first public electricity supply for the island. While it might look tempting to use the concrete steps at the edge of the railway line instead of the path, this is forbidden as the funicular carriage is considerably wider than the track.

As you near the bottom, the gradient eases and the path becomes grassy. Climb the small stile straight ahead to explore the shore on the right-hand side of the bay. At low tide there are impressive wave-cut platforms exposed, home to thousands of tiny mussels, winkles and anemones. To access the other side of the bay, pass through the gate next to the power station and follow the path directly in front of the turbine house before climbing another stile beyond. Cross the stream – this is usually straightforward. You can follow

a faint path along the shoreline all the way to the far end of the bay, passing the ruins of a house on the way.

The far end of the beach is the best place to find Jurassic fossils, particularly belemnites, ammonites and fossilised shells below an area of decaying cliffs. The area is a Site of Special Scientific Interest and fossils should not be removed by hammering, but can be taken if they are found loose amongst the pebbles on the beach. The bay is also a regular feeding spot for otters and diving birds, so fossil hunters should keep an eye on the sea as well. In the absence of a passenger-carrying scheme on the funicular railway, the only way back to the start is to return up the outward path.

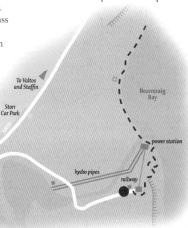

To Valtos and Staffin

Storr Car Park

Bearreraig Bay

power station

hydro pipes

railway

0   500m

bus stop

To Portree

Loch Leathan

The Old Man of Storr

Distance **3.5km** Time **2 hours**
Terrain **well-made paths, steep,
sometimes muddy** Map **OS Explorer 408**
Access **regular bus service (57) from
Portree passes the Storr car park**

**The most popular walk on Skye, the
iconic pinnacle of the Old Man of Storr
stands guard over the Sanctuary, a whole
array of fantastic rock formations
beneath the towering cliffs. This walk
climbs on a good path through the forest
to give a chance to explore this
remarkable place.**

From the busy car park on the forested
section of the A855 Portree to Staffin road,
take the path which starts through the
gate and heads uphill into the
plantations. The path twists up through

the forest, passing a clearing after a short
distance before climbing more steeply
and becoming rockier at times. Through
gaps in the trees there are good views
back over the Storr Lochs, which are
famed for their fly fishing, and over the
sea to the islands of Raasay and Rona.

Keep plodding uphill until the edge of
the forestry plantation is reached. Pass a
small pool on your left and go through
the gate with its intimidating warning
sign. From here you can see some of the
rock formations, including the Old Man
which can be hard to pick out at first
against the huge cliff of the Storr itself
towering behind. It can look particularly
dramatic when mist swirls around the
jutting rocks, exposing them to the eye
for fleeting glimpses.

◀ The Old Man of Storr

Keep going uphill on the clear path to a fork. Take the left-hand branch and follow it as it contours up the slope. When the path levels off and bends right just before a small depression, look out for another path going off to the right – remember this as it is used for the descent. First, though, continue ahead to get the best views of the Old Man. It was first climbed in 1955 by the late Don Whillans who achieved wider fame on the Alpine and Himalayan peaks. He described the Old Man's brittle and loose surface as like trying to climb up porridge.

If you continue on the main path it heads downhill into The Sanctuary, a hidden valley encircled by amazing formations. A warning sign marks where rockfalls have made it dangerous to continue behind the Old Man. In 2005 this area was the setting for a huge environmental artwork created by NVA, a Scottish arts company. Hundreds of visitors were led here by torchlight and the rocks were dramatically illuminated. There were live performances by the acclaimed local Gaelic singer Anne Martin and readings of the works of the poet Sorley MacLean together with other music and a spectacular light show.

On the return, take the path off to the left that was mentioned earlier. This crosses the slope well below the Old Man and eventually joins the outward path. If you want to explore further, turn left when you reach the main path and follow this uphill to the right of the Old Man and the Needle – a jagged tower with two holes through it. Eventually this path leads to a classic viewpoint looking back at the Old Man with the Storr Lochs in the background. Otherwise, follow the path downhill and back through the gate and the forestry to the car park.

Brothers' Point

Distance **3.5km** Time **1 hour 30**
Terrain **path with steep drops**
Map **OS Explorer 408** Access **regular bus
service (57) from Portree takes a circular
route around the Trotternish peninsula
– alight at Glenview Hotel, Culnacnoc**

**Rubha nam Brathairean is a dramatic
rocky spur jutting out into the sea.
A windswept but beautiful home to early
Celtic Christians hundreds of years ago,
it gives great coastal views up to the Kilt
Rock and waterfall, and across to the
islands of Rona and Raasay.**

At Culnacnoc, on the east side of the
Trotternish peninsula, there is parking in
a lay-by on the main road just north of

the Glenview Hotel. Head downhill a
short distance on the road before turning
left onto a track signed for Rubha nam
Brathairean (Gaelic for Brothers' Point).
Pass through a farm gate and continue
on the track until you pass a renovated
blackhouse on the right. Beyond this,
take the footpath marked 'to the shore'
which descends across grazing land
towards the sea, passing through a small
gate on the way. Just before you reach
the shore, there are the remains of a
settlement which once made the most
of this sheltered spot.

At the coast, turn right and cross the
outflow of the river before skirting the
edge of the pebbly shore. Here the

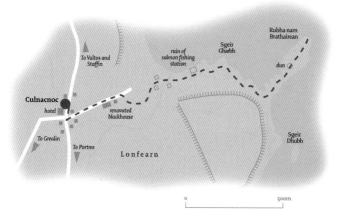

remains of a small square stone building nestle behind an outcrop of rock. This was a salmon fishing station, where the fish were brought ashore and processed before being sent in barrels to fishmarkets in London and Glasgow.

Continue up onto the grassy bank beyond and cross an area of boggy grass to follow the low cliff edge towards the point. The path soon reappears as it crosses a steep slope above a sea inlet – a head for heights is required as the steepness of the cliff is enhanced by the sight of various bits of sea flotsam – buoys, nets, fishermen's gloves etc that have washed up against the rocks below. Emerge onto a lovely green flat area with great views along the coast taking in the Kilt Rock to the north. Do not cross the stile, but instead follow the path along the side of the steep ridge which leads out

towards the point. The path climbs very steeply over Dun Hasan, the site of an Iron Age fort. The route up this is well-worn and easy to follow, but because of the sense of exposure you may need to use your hands to aid the ascent. Cross the top of the fort and follow the path down the other side – almost as steep – and out to the end of Brothers' Point. Here, faint oval-shaped depressions in the ground are thought to be the remains of basic cells or huts used by the early Christian settlers after whom the point is named. Although the views are spectacular, even in good weather it is hard to imagine how tough life must have been for these followers of Columba who sought to bring Christianity to these islands from their native Ireland. After exploring the point, retrace your steps to the start.

◀ The fort of Dun Hasan on Brothers' Point

Lealt and Loch Cuithir

**Distance 11km Time 2 hours 30
Terrain level track, optional very boggy
path Map OS Explorer 408 Access regular
bus service (57) runs from Portree and
can be taken in either direction as it
has a circular route around the
Trotternish peninsula**

**A walk exploring the industrial heritage
of the Trotternish peninsula. This
straightforward excursion visits the site
of diatomite workings from the early
20th century. It also offers close up views
of a little-visited but impressive part of
the Trotternish Ridge.**

Start the walk from the large lay-by at
Inver Tote on the seaward side of the A855
Portree to Staffin road. Cross the road and
walk uphill for 50 metres until you reach a
minor road to the left signed for Lealt.
Turn along this road with views of the

Trotternish Ridge ahead, its eastern side
an escarpment which runs almost from
the north end of the island all the way to
Portree. The ridge itself is 35km long and
its traverse is considered to be one of the
best in Scotland. It is usually tackled as a
two-day trek, although hardy souls and
hill runners have been known to complete
it considerably faster.

Looking down towards the Lealt River
on the left, you can clearly see the ridged
ground which is evidence of the run-rig
system of working the fields. At Lealt,
pass three houses before the road
becomes a track. Continue along it for
another 3.5km until it climbs slightly and
passes the brick remains of the diatomite
works to reach Loch Cuithir. From here
there are impressive views of the ridge,
especially the great towering prow of
Sgurr a'Mhadaidh Ruadh, the Hill of the
Red Fox, made famous in a children's
book by Allan Campbell McLean. Now a

peaceful spot, Loch Cuithir was a hive of activity in the late 19th and early 20th centuries. Diatomite, which is extracted from fossilised shells, was an important commodity at the time with many uses from the manufacture of dynamite to toothpaste. It was dredged from the bottom of the loch here and dried on wire mesh before being transported to Inver Tote on the coast along a railway. The railway was initially powered by human muscle and gravity alone until a steam locomotive was introduced in 1906. Both the railway and factory closed in 1915 as men left to fight in the First World War. The industry was briefly revived in the 1930s, but it soon closed for good, although there are still people living locally who can remember the diatomite works.

Loch Cuithir makes an ideal rest spot, with a picnic table close to the water's edge. The loch itself is home to whooper swans in the winter, whilst golden eagles

may be seen on the crags above.

The easiest return is to retrace your steps along the track and road. There is a very boggy alternative, which is to continue to where the track crosses a small stream and then head back on the rough, swampy ground on the far side. Once you are back in sight of the picnic table, bear right to pick up the beginning of the old railway. This can be followed until it rejoins the vehicle track about 1km further on; for the most part it is grassy, but several bridges are missing and inelegant muddy crossings of small streams are required. In places, the metal tracks are still intact and it is possible to imagine men toiling with heavy loads during the diatomite boom years.

Once back at the lay-by, follow the well-made path through the gate towards the coast, with views down into Lealt gorge. At the end of the path there is a viewpoint across the sea and an interpretative panel. Look down to the shore below to see the remains of the factory where the diatomite was ground and roasted before being shipped away from the island.

‹ Loch Cuithir with the Trotternish Ridge behind

An Corran – the dinosaur beach

Distance 4km Time 1 hour 30
Terrain rough moorland path, minor
roads Map OS Explorer 408
Access regular bus service (57) from
Portree takes a circular route around the
Trotternish peninsula

Staffin is a traditional crofting
community scattered around a lovely
bay, and remains a stronghold of the
Gaelic language. This walk follows the
old route to the slipway and visits a
beach where fossilised dinosaur
footprints were discovered in the 1980s.

Start the walk from the car park of
Columba 1400, the large white building
with the Celtic Cross on the front.
This houses a community and leadership
training centre providing courses for
disadvantaged young people and
businesses across the UK. Of more
interest to walkers, it also has an
excellent café. From the car park, follow
the gravel path uphill and turn right at
the sign for An Corran to join the path

that climbs beside a stone wall. This field
was part of the glebe land of the Church
of Scotland and was traditionally worked
by the community to provide upkeep for
the church and minister.

Cross the stile and climb up over the
moor until reaching the start of the steep
zigzagging descent to Staffin slipway seen
below. Look out for the remains of an Iron
Age chambered cairn just to the left of the
path. Behind are great views of the whole
Trotternish Ridge from the Storr to the
Quiraing, whilst on a clear day the
mainland hills of Torridon and Applecross
can be seen over the sea ahead. Follow the
distinct path down the zigzags and
continue to the slipway on the shore,
taking care as the path can be slippery
when wet.

After exploring the slipway, head left
along the coast road. At the lay-by, take the
ramp down to the small sandy beach at An
Corran. At low tide, fossilised dinosaur
footprints are sometimes exposed to the
right of the large boulders on the flat mud

◀ Looking across Staffin Bay towards the Quiraing

stone. The footprints probably belong to the Megalosaurus, a carnivore which grew up to 10 metres long and lived in the area 165 million years ago. Paleontologists say that the way the footprints of adults and young are clustered together may be evidence that dinosaurs actively reared their young. After studying them for yourselves, you may conclude that they were just having a game of Twister! The first dinosaur fossils in Scotland were found in this area in 1982. Replicas of the most important finds can be seen in the excellent Staffin Museum (by the Kilt Rock). Run by a local crofter who doubles as a knowledgeable dinosaur enthusiast, the museum also houses a number of other local finds including the fossil leg-bone of a large Diplodocus-type dinosaur. This creature was a herbivore, feasting on Jurassic vegetation until it reached 18 metres in length.

An Corran was also home to an important Mesolithic community. Stone tools made here have been found in Applecross and other sites around the Inner Sound, suggesting that An Corran may have been a hub of trade and sea traffic. The main part of the site was buried when the road to the slipway was constructed, although a protective layer of sand was placed on top of the site to allow for future archaeological exploration. Just offshore is Staffin Island with the remains of its salmon fishing station and the poles used for drying nets; today the island is used only for grazing cattle in the winter months. The beasts swim across guided by rope at neep tides.

Continue along the coast road to a cattle grid and bridge over the Stenscholl River. Both sides of the bridge are good places to look for otters, particularly towards where the river meets the sea. Keep left, following the road up the hill to the T-junction with the main road. Cross the road and turn left along the pavement to return to Columba 1400, passing Staffin Stores on the right.

Bioda Buidhe

Distance **2km** Time **1 hour** Terrain **faint moorland path** Map **OS Explorer 408** Access **regular bus service (57) from Portree passes the end of the crosscountry Staffin to Uig road 3km from the start of the walk**

This short but steep walk follows part of the Trotternish Ridge, an impressive escarpment that runs from the north of the island to Portree. It has great views over the best and most popular bits of the ridge, the Quiraing and the Storr, whilst avoiding the crowds. You may enjoy sightings of golden eagles as well as views across to the mainland and the islands of Raasay and Rona.

The walk starts from the parking area for the Quiraing at the top of the hairpin bends on the crosscountry road from Staffin to Uig. Here you can look down at the switchback of the road and the scattered white houses of Staffin. Take the path on the same side of the road as the parking area to immediately cross a burn and follow the rough, eroded path as it starts climbing uphill (the path on the other side of the road is the popular route taken to explore the pinnacles and strange rock features of the Quiraing).

As you climb, keep close to the cliff edge on your left. The view of the Quiraing behind becomes more impressive, whilst looking down

there are a number of rocky stacks and small lochans, all formed from the landslip movements of the escarpment which is gradually heading seawards. You can also make out the rectangular shapes of old peat cutting areas far below. Although these peat bogs are no longer used to cut fuel commercially, there are areas of Trotternish where people do still cut and dry peat to use for heating.

Soon you reach the first summit jutting out from the line of the cliff edge, in fine weather a perfect grassy spot for a picnic. This is the point from which many walkers return to the car park, but it is well worth continuing to the true top of Bioda Buidhe. It is necessary to head to the right away from the edge at this point to avoid a steep drop. There are a number of faint sheep paths, but as long as you keep a safe distance from the cliff edge you can descend a little and cross a flatter area before heading uphill onto the escarpment edge once more: follow this to the top.

From the summit of Bioda Buidhe you can see almost the entire length of the Trotternish Ridge and should be able to make out the prominent peak of the Storr

towards Portree. The high crags here are frequented by golden eagles and it is worth walking the whole length of the flat summit area to ensure you don't miss anything.

The return is by the same route. Although it is tempting to cut down direct to the parking area, this route is often boggy and it is usually easier to stick to the outward route closer to the cliff edge.

◄ From Bioda Buidhe looking towards the Quiraing

19

The Quiraing

Distance 4.5km Time 2 hours
Terrain rocky path with steep slopes
Map OS Explorer 408 Access regular bus
service (57) from Portree passes the
Flodigarry end of the walk

This spectacular walk takes you into
the heart of the Quiraing, a fantastic
landscape of rocky pinnacles, cliffs and
hidden green swards. The walk can be
done as a one-way through route if
transport allows; otherwise you can
begin at the pass for an easier walk or
the Flodigarry end for a tougher one,
returning the same way once you
reach the Prison.

Start at the parking area at the top of the
pass, just above the hairpin bends on the
Staffin to Uig high road. Here you are on
the edge of the escarpment that makes up
the Trotternish Ridge – a 36km eroding
landslip that creates an impressive
geographic divide across this
northern peninsula of the

island. Cross the road and take the clear and
flat path on the other side, signed for
Flodigarry. There are good views down
across Staffin Bay and on a clear day you can
see the mountains on the mainland and the
houses of Gairloch directly opposite.

Follow the path as it heads towards the
pinnacles that make up the weird
landscape of the Quiraing. The path
traverses a very steep slope and at one
point crosses a small gully with a short,
awkward rocky section that requires care.

The path beyond continues to contour
along the slope and soon the impressive
rock feature of the Prison comes into view
straight ahead. This towering rocky
landform has been the scene of numerous
accidents to those trying to scale its three
summits made up of loose rock. Continue
on the path slightly uphill into the
gap between the Prison and the
main mass of the Quiraing. High
up ahead is the Needle, a
prominent detached pinnacle;

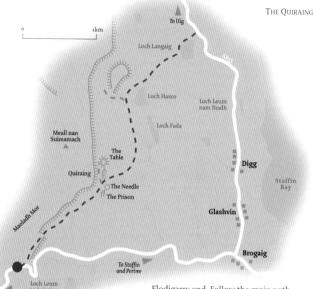

0 ___ 1km

To Uig
Loch Langaig
Loch Hasco
Loch Leum
nam Bradh
Loch Fada
Meall nan
Suireamach
The
Table
Quiraing
The Needle
The Prison
Digg
Staffin
Bay
Glashvin
Maolach Mor
Brogaig
To Staffin
and Portree
Loch Leum
na Luirginn
To Uig

beyond the Needle but out of sight is the Table, a flat grassy area in the middle of the Quiraing surrounded by rocky towers. Reaching the Table involves heading up and down some very steep, eroded ground and requires great care, particularly in descent, so it is best left to experienced hillwalkers. Local folklore claims that people used to hide cattle there when raiders were spotted, and that games of shinty were sometimes played on the top, but it doesn't say how the ball was retrieved when it was hit over the edge.

If returning to the car park, turn back here, but if transport allows you can continue the walk through to the Flodigarry end. Follow the main path ahead, descending slightly and passing under a rocky overhang and then continuing across the slopes. Where the path forks, keep to the right and follow the route downhill. Eventually you pass to the left of Loch Hasco in a deep fold of the hills, and, further down, Loch Langaig. There is a good picnic or rest spot on the grassy ground near the outflow of the loch. There are great views out across the sea, with Flodigarry Island in the foreground, a breeding spot for puffins. Just beyond Loch Langaig is the road, with a parking area a short distance along it to the left. This road is on the main bus route to Uig and Portree with the official bus stop a little way north along the road towards Flodigarry.

Rubha Hunish

Distance 7km **Time** 3 hours **Terrain** boggy, indistinct path across moorland **Map** OS Explorer 408 **Access** regular bus service (57) from Portree takes a circular route around the Trotternish peninsula passing Duntulm

Rubha Hunish is the most northerly part of the island, an unexpectedly dramatic headland and an unmissable walk on a fine day. With spectacular views to the Outer Hebrides, impressive cliffs, abundant wildlife and a deserted village, this walk has everything for the more adventurous walker wanting to experience a hidden part of Skye.

From the A855 which curves around the north end of the island between Staffin and Kilmuir, take the turning for Shulista next to a red telephone box. A gravel car park is almost immediately reached on the right. Cross the cattle grid and then take the faint path going off to the left.

It becomes clearer and heads towards the gap in the hills seen ahead. Although faint at times, the path follows the line of a small escarpment and keeps in the same northerly direction. After a while, the ruins of Erisco village and Duntulm Castle come into view on the left.

The path heads through a kissing gate in a wire fence, crosses a boggy patch and then carries on uphill. Keep right at the fork and continue to climb until a small square building comes into view. This is the old coastguard lookout and is now maintained by volunteers from the Mountain Bothies Association. It is an open shelter and is a great spot to have a rest and set up binoculars to watch for wildlife, especially whales, dolphins and porpoises passing the headland of Rubha Hunish which is in view far below. Please help maintain the shelter by carrying out any rubbish you find here.

After leaving the lookout, follow the

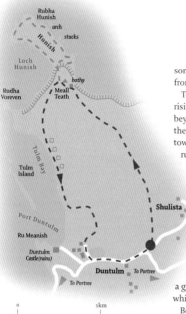

some may prefer just to admire the view from the top.

To continue the walk, follow the path rising out of the dip and over the heather beyond. It curves round, keeping close to the line of the cliffs, and then descends towards Tulm bay with its island and the ruins of the castle and the white hotel straight ahead. At the bottom of the hill, pass through a wooden gate and follow the faint path as it skirts along the shoreline between the sea and the row of ruined houses which once made up the village of Erisco. Along the shore, look for the bright green hummocks which mark the territory of local otters. This bay is a great place to spot them swimming, whilst seals can also sometimes be seen.

Before reaching a stone wall follow a faint path diagonally inland, aiming for a corner of the wall to where it becomes a wire fence. Cross the small stile over this, and keep right alongside the wall before going through the first gate on the right. Turn left after the gate, passing a small house on the right and joining a track. Follow this to the left, passing in front of a row of houses which were once the home of the coastguards who manned the lookout. Continue on the track, taking the left-hand fork and climbing up to the main road. Turn left on the road and follow it past a small loch and a house to the telephone box and the start of the walk.

path to the left as you look out to sea; soon it descends steeply into a wide dip. At the far end of the dip, there is a large boulder right on the edge of the cliffs. This marks the top of the path down to the Hunish headland itself. The path looks daunting from the top, but the descent is easier than it appears and makes a fantastic optional detour (allow an extra hour) for those who want closer encounters with the seabirds, wildlife and cliffs with sea stacks, arches and deep tidal geos on the coast far below. It does, however, require a head for heights and

◄ Looking down on Rubha Hunish

The Cave of Gold

Distance **2.5km** Time **1 hour 30**
Terrain **boggy fields, very steep descent
to the sea** Map **OS Explorer 408**
Access **regular bus (57) from Portree
passes along the A855 through Kilmuir –
get off at the road junction for Camas
Mor, 2km from the start**

**Visit Skye's answer to Fingal's Cave on
Staffa – the Cave of Gold (Uamh Oir in
Gaelic), surrounded by hexagonal basalt
columns. This hidden spot makes the
perfect place to sunbathe or watch for
whales and other sealife.**

This walk is near the tip of the dramatic
Trotternish Peninsula. Take the road
signed for Camas Mor from the A855;
follow the second sign for Camas Mor if
heading north from Uig. Just after the
road passes a ruined church, take the next
turning on the right. Drive to the end of
the road where there is room to park: take
care not to block any gates or the turning
circle. Start the walk in the same direction
as the road across croftland towards the
coast. The land here is used for grazing
cattle and sheep, so dogs should be kept
on short leads. Head slightly towards the
left to follow the inland side of a fence,
which is broken down in places.

The high cliffs are impressive here and
soon a deep inlet or geo cuts inland.
Continue along the fenceline, passing
through the remains of an old stone wall,
until a farm gate and a kissing gate are
reached. Go through the kissing gate and

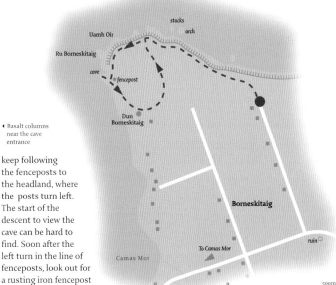

◂ Basalt columns
near the cave
entrance

keep following
the fenceposts to
the headland, where
the posts turn left.
The start of the
descent to view the
cave can be hard to
find. Soon after the
left turn in the line of
fenceposts, look out for
a rusting iron fencepost
set into a boulder. Taking
great care, make a very steep
descent down the grass slope to the
coast here, keeping the crags just to
your right. It can be very slippery after
rain. Two thirds of the way down, you'll
reach a wide rocky platform – go along
this to the right.

The cave entrance is visible just round
the corner. It is not possible to enter the
cave but this is a delightful spot, with
perfect hexagonal columns of basalt all
around. There are usually lots of shags
and other seabirds nearby, and it is worth
keeping an eye out for dolphins,
porpoises or basking sharks offshore.
Return up the grassy slope to the clifftop

and follow it to the right along a faint
path. From here, the views to the Outer
Hebrides are magnificent on a clear day.

As the scattered houses of Kilmuir come
into view in the distance, the rocky hillock
of Dun Borneskitaig rises in the
foreground. This ruinous iron-age broch
was used as a defensive shelter against
Norse raiders. Before reaching the broch,
bear left along the remains of a low stone
dyke and then, still heading left, aim
towards the sea by the fence. Soon the
kissing gate from earlier in the walk is
reached. Go through this to retrace your
steps along the cliffs to the start.

Hugh's Castle

Distance **4.5km** Time **1 hour 30**
Terrain **waymarked rough path**
Map **OS Explorer 408** Access **regular bus service (57) from Portree takes a circular route around the Trotternish peninsula – this passes the start of the road down to Cuidrach.**

Hugh's Castle – the last medieval fortress to be built on Skye – is little visited today, but this walk is well worthwhile to enjoy the views over Loch Snizort to the Waternish peninsula and the tiny islands scattered between.

The walk starts from Cuidrach, on the western side of the Trotternish peninsula. The road is signed from the A87, but be sure not to take the more southerly turning to South Cuidrach. There is parking in a disused quarry on the right-hand side of the road just under 1km from the junction with the A87. There is sometimes further parking at the bottom of the road, but this is very limited. Walk down the road but, before you reach the houses and shore, veer to the left along a track signposted for Caisteal Uisdean. The track passes two houses, the second one with a distinctive red roof. Here the track ends and a path begins, keeping close to the wire fence and then bearing slightly right. There are wooden marker posts with carved Celtic symbols at intervals along the route; keep a careful eye out for them as the path is unclear.

After a stile, the path turns downhill

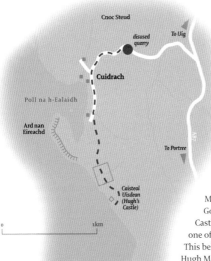

Cnoc Steud

disused quarry

To Uig

Cuidrach

Poll na h-Ealaidh

Ard nan Eireachd

To Portree

Caisteal Uisdean (Hugh's Castle)

0   1km

Am Bagh-dhuin

square of stone that is Caisteal Uisdean. The castle was built in the 17th century when the sea was the main thoroughfare. The door was on an upper floor and would have been accessed via a retractable wooden stairway.

The keep was built by Hugh MacDonald, cousin to Donald Gorm Mor of nearby Duntulm Castle. Some claim that the castle is one of the most haunted in Scotland. This belief stems from the gory death of Hugh MacDonald in the dungeon of Duntulm. Trying to arrange to have his cousin murdered, Hugh wrote two letters, one inviting his cousin to a meal and another hiring an assassin to kill him. The two letters got mixed up and Donald imprisoned Hugh in Duntulm dungeon, feeding him only on salt beef and providing no water until Hugh lost his mind and finally died from the thirst.

In today's more peaceful times, the surrounding cliffs are a good place for birdwatching and in winter the neighbouring fields offer temporary home to migrating greylag geese. The return to Cuidrach is by the same outward path. If a longer walk is required, then a path heading north from Cuidrach leads to the crofting settlement of Earlish, from which you can either retrace your steps or return via the road.

towards an inlet. On the headland opposite, the small ridged patterns in the earth are evidence that the area was once worked in lazy-beds where the strips of earth were raised to dry out with drainage channels between. Many of the implements used to work the soil and cut the seaweed for use on the beds as fertiliser can be seen at the nearby Museum of Island Life. The sheer size and weight of these implements show that there was nothing lazy about cultivating lazy-beds, and the photos reveal that much of the work was done by women.

Climb a second stile and cross the field diagonally, heading towards the imposing

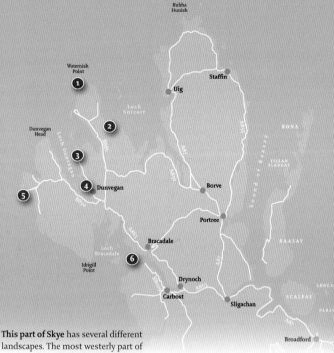

This part of Skye has several different landscapes. The most westerly part of Skye, Duirinish, has one of Britain's most dramatic sections of coastline, from cliffs over 300 metres high near Neist Point to the beautiful Claigan coral beaches. Inland is a wild moorland where the strange flat-topped summits of MacLeod's Tables dominate the landscape, whilst Dunvegan and its ancient castle guards the routes into the peninsula.

Waternish is a smaller, more intimate crofting landscape. This area has been revived in recent years as many artists and craftspeople have moved here and set up studios. At its heart is the picturesque but tiny village of Stein. The Waternish coastline may be less dramatic than that of Duirinish, but it has sweeping seascapes and the chance to watch for whales or dolphins.

South of Dunvegan, the area around Struan has some of Skye's finest views across Loch Harport to the Cuillin. The gem here is the tidal island of Oronsay withs its wonderful views, sea stacks and arches.

Dunvegan and Northwest Skye

1 **Waternish Point**   30
Journey through some of Skye's
bloody clan history on the way to
visit a lonesome lighthouse

2 **The Cliffs of Score Horan**   32
Golden eagles are among the few
visitors to this wilder side of the
Waternish peninsula

3 **Claigan coral beaches**   34
No need to rush down in the
morning with your beachtowel to
reserve a spot on this sandy stretch

4 **The Two Churches Walk**   36
An enjoyable stroll through
woods and over moorland above
Dunvegan Castle

5 **Neist Point Lighthouse**   38
Go west for stunning views,
excellent birdwatching and the
chance of spotting passing whales

6 **Oronsay Island**   40
Explore the rock features and sea
stacks around Loch Bracadale and
enjoy good views across to Minginish

Waternish Point

Distance 13.5km Time 4 hours
Terrain boggy track, pathless grassy coast
Map OS Explorer 407 Access no regular
bus service to Trumpan

**The lighthouse at lonely Waternish Point
is a place of wide seascapes, and the walk
out to it passes several interesting
historical remains.**

There is a parking area opposite the
ruins of Trumpan Church. Though today
a peaceful spot with picnic tables and a
view of Ardmore Point, the sad ruins are
testament to one of the most notorious
episodes in Skye's history. One Sunday in
1578 the local MacLeods were gathered for
worship in this church. The MacDonalds,
of whom 395 had been massacred in a
cave on Eigg at the hands of the MacLeods
the previous year, had arrived from Uist
and landed in Ardmore Bay. They
barricaded the doors of the packed church
and set fire to the thatch. All the
worshippers were burned alive, save for
one young girl who managed to escape
through a tiny window. The girl ran to
raise the alarm, and the MacLeods
responded. Their famous totem, the Fairy
Flag (which has the power to save the clan
three times), was unveiled and an army of
MacLeods massacred the MacDonalds in
turn. The bodies were dumped in a nearby
dyke, giving the incident the grisly name
'The Spoiling of the Dyke'.

Coming out of the parking area, turn
left back along the road, passing some
houses, to where it bends right 500m
away. Turn left through a gate onto a
track. Around 2km further, a cairn is
reached on the left, commemorating the

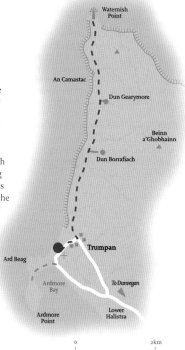

death of a Roderick MacLeod who died nearby in an earlier battle between the two clans in 1530. A little further on, the track crosses a bridge and becomes very boggy for a short stretch; it is easier to walk along the moor to the left to avoid this. A large ruinous stone structure is visible well above the track to the right. This is Dun Borrafiach, an Iron Age broch or defensive tower. It is worth detouring across the rough ground to visit it as it is one of the best preserved examples on the island, with its walls of massive stone blocks still standing over 3 metres tall.

Returning to the track, continue ahead. Another broch, Dun Gearymore, becomes visible on a grassy mound to the right. This may look more ruinous than Dun Borrafiach, but an easy detour to it reveals a short section of passageway with its roof remaining intact. After cresting a low hill, a small lighthouse becomes visible far ahead. As the track bends right, head diagonally down across the heather and grass towards the coast, passing through a gap in an old drystone wall halfway down. Beyond, continue across the grassy slopes above the cliffs, dotted with lazybeds – ridged undulations in the grass that are the remains of cultivation. The clifftop walk carries on all the way to the lighthouse, which is solar powered and completely automatic. This is a great place for a picnic, with superb seascapes stretching

from Dunvegan Head to Trotternish and taking in the Outer Hebrides all the way from South Uist to Lewis. In July and August, watch out for minke whales which can often be seen feeding just off the point.

Although it is possible to continue round the other side of the coast to Geary, this is very hard going – requiring a full day – and the only easy option is to return by the outward route.

‹ Dunvegan Head seen from the walk to Waternish Point

The Cliffs of Score Horan

Distance **5km** Time **1 hour 30**
Terrain **forestry track, boggy moorland
path** Map **OS Explorer 407** Access **no
regular bus service to Gillen**

**This circular route explores the little-
visited eastern side of the Waternish
peninsula. The craggy escarpment of
Score Horan is the highlight, where the
cliffs of Beinn an Sguirr plunge down
to the sea.**

Start the walk from the road end at
Gillen, where there is room to park
without blocking the turning area. Go
through the gate at the end of the road,
and continue on the track across the
fields ahead, ignoring two turnings on the
left before passing through a further gate.
The track enters a forestry plantation.
Ignore another turning to the left at an
old quarry and instead continue straight
ahead. Soon the track emerges from the
forest and runs along the edge of a
recently felled area with open ground to
the right. Just before it begins to descend,
turn left onto another track back into the
trees. This climbs gently and reaches the
open moor near another quarry.

Continue on the track with extensive
views of the moorland over which hen
harriers can sometimes be seen. Climbing
up the track towards the skyline, look out
for a wooden post marking the start of the
footpath to the cliff. Turn left here and

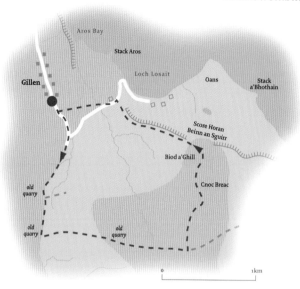

take the usually wet path as it contours around Cnoc Breac. Follow the marker posts and eventually the path heads downhill and towards the cliff edge. From this vantage point the impressive cliffs of Beinn an Sguirr can be enjoyed. With their fortified appearance and crumbling rocks which are uninviting to climbers, these crags are a favourite haunt of golden eagles.

The path dips slightly away from the vertigo-inducing cliff edge to follow a narrow route downhill through pine trees, emerging again at the cliffs further on. Below the bay of Loch Losait can be seen, with the ruins of houses now providing shelter for sheep near the shore. Further

out into Loch Snizort lie the Ascrib Isles and beyond them Trotternish Ridge in the distance.

Keep on the faint path as it descends near the edge of the cliff, watching out for the ravines which give Gillen its Norse name. Eventually, the path passes through an area of felled trees onto a track. Turn right here and then immediately left. If you want to explore the old settlement at the bottom of the bay, take the track heading right and follow it downhill. Otherwise accompany the track for a short distance and go through the second gate on the right, taking the old grassy track back to the road end at Gillen.

◄ Loch Losait from the cliffs of Score Horan

Claigan coral beaches

Distance 4km Time 1 hour 30
Terrain track, grassy path
Map OS Explorer 407 Access no regular
bus service to Claigan; Dunvegan, and
bus (56) to Portree, is 6km away

**A taste of the Carribean on Skye, even in
dull weather the coral beaches seem to
shine brilliant white. They are a great
place to explore, picnic, collect seashells
or, for the brave, swim. This is an easy
and very popular walk with only a couple
of short uphill sections.**

The walk starts at the car park at the
road end at Claigan, northwest of
Dunvegan. Take the track from the end of
the parking area towards the sea. Follow
it as it bends right and runs parallel to
the coast; one section is sometimes wet

but it can be crossed with stepping
stones. The track passes nearer to the
shore and there are good views across
Loch Dunvegan with the flat tops of
MacLeod's Tables visible in the distance.
Soon a pebbly bay with a small amount
of coral sand at low tide is reached. The
track heads away to the right here.
Continue instead on a grassy footpath
aiming for a clear gap in the drystone
wall, crossing a small stream on the way.

After passing through the wall, carry on
over the rise and when you reach the top
there is a view across to the coral beaches.
The indistinct path crosses the short-
cropped grass and heads straight for the
beach. The sand is actually made up from
maerl, the calcified remains of a type of
seaweed that grows in beds off the coast.

▲ Coral beach and the island of Lampay

The particles get smaller the further across the beach you walk, and there are also hundreds of tiny but beautiful snail shells. The sand is alkaline and used to be used by local crofters to treat acid peat soils far from the beach. The island just off the shore to the left is Lampay and the larger island straight ahead is Isay; Lampay can be reached at very low tides. It is well worth ascending the little flat-topped hill behind the beaches, known as Cnoc Mor a' Ghrobain, before leaving. This has excellent extensive views over the beaches from Stein in Waternish right round to Dunvegan Head. The return is by the same route.

Map labels:
Groban na Sgeire
Lovaig Bay
Cnoc Mor a' Ghrobain
Lampay
An Dornell
coral beaches
Claigan
pebble beach
Rudha na Gairbhe
0   500m
To Dunvegan

The Two Churches Walk

Distance **3km** Time **1 hour** Terrain **good
paths, sometimes muddy**
Map **OS Explorer 407** Access **regular bus
service (56) from Portree to Dunvegan**

**This circular route from Dunvegan is
popular with locals as well as visitors.
It gives a mix of open moor and
pleasant woodland, with glimpses of
Dunvegan Castle.**

Start at the ruin of St Mary's Church on
the Portree road out of Dunvegan, where
there is a lay-by for parking. The ruins
that you can see today stand on the site of
a much older Celtic site probably dating
back to the time when St Columba left
Ireland to spread Christianity to Skye and
the other islands. The churchyard is the
final resting place of many old local
families including five chiefs of the
Macleod clan from Dunvegan Castle.

After exploring the ruin and churchyard
take the gravel path in front of the
churchyard wall and around to the right
of the ruin. Climbing gently uphill, you
can see a memorial plaque on the wall of

the church commemorating the graves of
the MacCrimmons, the hereditary pipers
to Clan MacLeod.

Follow the clear path up past a sheep
fank used for dipping, sorting and
shearing the sheep. At the top of the
enclosure you reach a gate. Here you can
detour to the Duirinish standing stone
visible over to the left, which has fine
views over Loch Dunvegan and the village
itself to the strange flat-topped hills of
MacLeod's Tables. To reach the stone, turn
left just before the gate and cross the

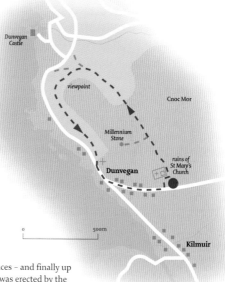

grassy field – wet in places – and finally up the hill to the stone. It was erected by the local community to celebrate the turn of the millennium. The stone weighs about five tonnes and was pulled into place using a system of ropes and pulleys – and the combined muscle power of Duirinish. A time capsule was placed beneath it for future generations to unearth.

Returning to the gate, pass through it and continue uphill on the path as it crosses over the common grazing for the local area. Go through a second gate as the path begins to descend through woodland with glimpses of Dunvegan Castle through the trees; keep left at the fork. The path widens and after a short while you need to look for a turning to the left onto a narrower but clear path.

If you reach the road you have gone too far and should to go back.

Soon the woods thin out and there is an excellent viewpoint for Dunvegan Castle and the many islands in the loch. Beyond this, the woodland becomes a dense plantation with spruces blocking out the light. It comes as a surprise, therefore, when you emerge into the light at the striking white structure of Duirinish Parish Church. From the church turn left onto the road and follow it, keeping left at the next junction, back to the start of the walk.

◄ The Duirinish stone, above Dunvegan

Neist Point Lighthouse

Distance **2km** Time **1 hour 30**
Terrain **well-made path with steps**
Map **OS Explorer 407** Access **regular bus
service (56) from Portree to Glendale,
5km from start of walk**

**Neist Point is the westernmost headland
on Skye and its dramatically situated
lighthouse can feel like the very edge of
the world. It offers an easy walk with
excellent views both of the coastal cliffs
and the Outer Hebrides. The seas around
Neist are ferocious on a stormy day, but
in fine weather this is a great place for
seabirds and whale-spotting.**

Take the Milovaig road from Glendale
signed for Neist Point. There is a parking
area at the very end of the road. To begin
the walk to the lighthouse, go through
the gate and follow the concrete path.
It soon begins to descend, with steps and
a handrail at the steepest parts. Over to
the right is an old aerial rope-way system
which was built to take supplies out to
the lighthouse cottages. These days the
lighthouse is still in use but is fully
automatic, and the cottages where the
lighthouse keepers lived are now privately
owned holiday rentals.

After the descent, the path passes
to the left of the grassy hill of
An t-Aigeach (meaning the Stallion).
The other side of this hill is a dramatic
upstanding sea cliff and the site of some
of Skye's hardest rock climbs. The top of
the cliffs can be reached by detouring up
to the right here, but there is no path and
most continue towards the lighthouse.

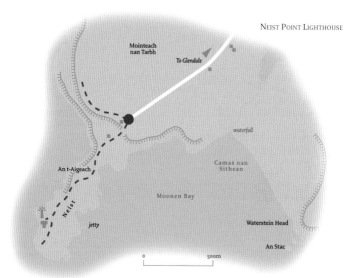

There are great views behind of the impressive wall of Waterstein Head, the second highest coastal cliff on Skye.

The path ends just before the lighthouse and cottages which are on fenced private land. The complex was built in 1909 at a cost of £4350 – the engineer being David A Stevenson of the famous Stevenson family of lighthouse builders. More recently, several scenes in Lars Von Trier's harrowing film *Breaking the Waves*, starring Emily Lloyd, were shot here and for several years a cemetery which had been constructed as part of the film set was left in place as an eerie memento, most visitors to Neist presuming it to be genuine.

The area to the left of the lighthouse is well worth exploring for its hexagonal basalt rock formations. The point is also

an excellent place for watching seabirds, with gannets, black guillemots, razorbills and shags usually plentiful, as well as being one of the best locations on Skye for spotting whales and dolphins. Minke whales are very frequent visitors here in the summer and basking sharks and even killer whales have been spotted. Return to the car park by the same route.

Before leaving, it is worth walking out along the clifftop to the north of the car park for the classic view of the lighthouse. Head up the rough ground behind the store building and continue west to reach the cliff edge, following this to the north. Soon the lighthouse comes into view beyond the cliffs of An t-Aigeach, making a perfect composition for photographers. There can be few better places to watch the sunset.

◀ Neist Point Lighthouse and the cliffs of An t-Aigeach

Oronsay Island

Distance 5km **Time** 2 hours
Terrain boggy paths, pebbly tidal
causeway **Map** OS Explorer 407 **Access**
limited bus service (56A) from Portree to
Dunvegan, stops at Ullinish Hotel

*Oronsay can only be reached at low tide; you
must check the tide times before setting out
on this walk and ensure you have enough time
to return from the island. Portree Tourist
Information Centre has tide timetables, or
you can check them on the internet.*

**Venture onto a tidal island and explore
the high sea cliffs, arches and caves
of its coastline. Oronsay Island juts out
into Loch Bracadale, a picturesque sea
loch scattered with islets on the west
side of Skye.**

Follow the signs for Ullinish House
Hotel at the turning from the A863
Sligachan to Dunvegan road. After 2km
branch off this minor road to the left,
following a sign for Oronsay Path. There
is parking at the very end of this road.
A further footpath sign marked 'Oronsay
via tidal causeway' indicates the start of
the walk, heading through a gate. Almost
immediately, pass through a kissing gate
and follow the track across the field.

At the far end of the field, the path goes
through another gate and curves round
just above the sea. There are great views
of Tarner Island with its impressive arch
to the north. The route gently ascends the
hill ahead and crosses a boggy area to
reach another gate with a view of Oronsay
across the tidal narrows below. Go
through the gate and descend the path to
the shore. The clear, shallow waters of

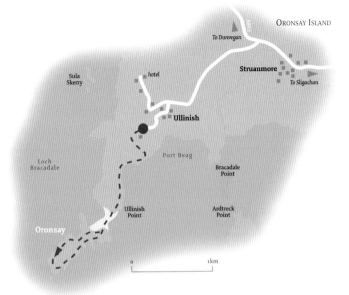

To Dunvegan

Struanmore

To Sligachan

hotel

Sula
Skerry

Ullinish

Loch
Bracadale

Port Beag

Bracadale
Point

Oronsay

Ullinish
Point

Ardtreck
Point

0   1km

Loch Bracadale make it a popular area for mussel farms and scallop diving; it is also well known for its crabs.

Oronsay is a Norse word meaning a tidal island; there are at least 20 Oronsays or Ornsays in the Hebrides, including two on Skye. The stony causeway giving access to it is completely covered at high tide, and it is best to head across as the tide is still going out to give yourself plenty of time to explore the island before returning.

Once across the causeway, the walking on Oronsay itself is on delightfully dry turf. The main path heads straight towards the prominent cliff edges on the north side of the island. Follow this path to the far end of Oronsay, detouring on sheep paths to visit the high points of

the cliffs for great views of the other islands in Loch Bracadale and across to the Minginish coastline. At the furthest point, you can look down on some sea stacks far below. Return the way you came for 100m or so until you can descend easily to the lower southerly coast of the island. At first sight, this is less dramatic than the northern cliffs; however, there are many intricate rock features. After 500m, you reach a deep inlet carved by the sea. Walk around it and, once on the far side, look back along the coastline to see a remarkable tunnel-like arch cut through the cliffs.

The path round the south coast eventually leads back to the tidal causeway which you cross to retrace your steps to the start of the walk.

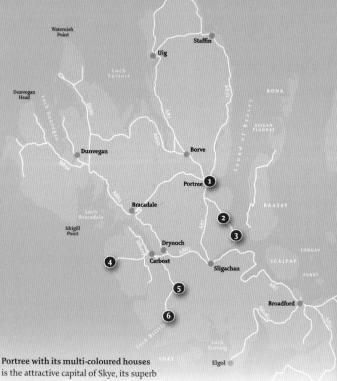

Portree with its multi-coloured houses
is the attractive capital of Skye, its superb
natural harbour busy with boats. It is the
gateway to the Braes, a peaceful and very
beautiful crofting landscape with some
superb coastal scenery.

The main road south is dominated
by the Cuillin, the most spectacular
and challenging mountains in Britain.
These airy spires are a mecca for rock
climbers and scramblers, but around
their base there are easier walks that
enable less experienced walkers to
appreciate their drama close at hand in the
bowls of Coire Lagan and the Fairy Pools
of Coire na Creiche.

Immediately north of these peaks
are the wild moors and coastline of
Minginish, with Talisker Bay a perfect
sandy haven breaking up the line of cliffs.
There are further beaches at Fiskavaig,
whilst the village of Carbost is home to
the Talisker whisky distillery.

Central Skye

1 **Scorrybreac circuit**   44
Be on the look-out for sea eagles on the cliffs below Ben Tianavaig as you leave bustling Portree behind

2 **Coille Iosal and the Braes**   46
Head south from Portree to explore a fertile part of Skye made famous by a rebellion of evicted crofters

3 **An Aird Peninsula**   48
Explore the cliffs, look out for seals and enjoy the seabird colonies of this easily reached promontory

4 **Talisker Bay**   50
Round off a visit to a deservedly popular beach with a wee dram at the nearby distillery

5 **The Fairy Pools**   52
Get close to the peaks of the Cuillin without getting too high on this entertaining circuit

6 **Coire Lagan and the Eas Mor**   54
A journey into the thrilling heart of the Cuillin: an extension of the route will suit walkers keen on scrambling

Scorrybreac circuit

Distance 3km **Time** 1 hour 30
Terrain waymarked path with a short,
steep ascent **Map** OS Explorer 410
Access buses serve Portree from all parts
of the island

**This picturesque and straightforward
coastal circuit has great views of Portree
Harbour and the coastline. A path along
the shore gives good opportunities for
encounters with seals and, if you are
lucky, sea eagles, before climbing
through woodland to return past the
Cuillin Hills Hotel.**

From the centre of Portree, follow the
road above the harbour signed for
Staffin. Take the first right turn and head
downhill along Scorrybreac Road. There is
parking just after the turning to the
Cuillin Hills Hotel. The walk begins along
the tarmac path close to the wooded
shore. Looking back, there are excellent
views of the brightly coloured cottages
around Portree Harbour. Behind them is a
wooded area, known locally as 'the Lump',
which is where the annual Highland
Games are held. The prominent tower is
an Apothecary's tower, built as a sign to
passing seafarers that medical assistance
was available in the village.

Pass the boathouse, which is home to
Portree Sailing Club, before crossing a
footbridge and reaching a gate signed
'Urras Clann Mhicneacail'. This is Gaelic
for the Nicolson Trust; the headland
beyond has been purchased by members

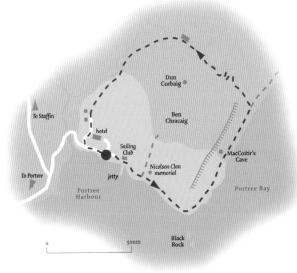

of the Clan Nicolson overseas, Scorrybreac being considered the homeland of the clan. To the left, after the gate, is a Clan memorial with flagpoles and grand views across Loch Portree to the distant Cuillin mountains.

Continue on the now rougher path beside the shore. Part of the Isle of Raasay can be seen ahead, whilst the hill across the bay is Ben Tianavaig. Sea eagles (also known as white-tailed eagles) often nest on the steep cliffs below Ben Tianavaig, so watch out for them fishing in the bay. The outcrop just offshore, which can be reached at low tide, is the Black Rock. A little further on there is a salmon farm just offshore. You may see the

fish as they jump up from the water.

At the corner of the bay, the path reaches a stone seat from where the high coastal cliffs to the north are revealed. The going becomes stonier at this point; continue until the path reaches a drystone wall. Turn left and follow the path uphill, at first beside the wall; soon it bends left and ascends a steep series of zigzags. Above these, the route levels off and crosses more open land. Pass through a kissing gate before heading downhill to a further gate. The route now enters an attractive silver birch wood. Descend along the edge of the wood to emerge behind the Cuillin Hills Hotel. The tarmac drive leads back to Scorrybreac Road.

◀ Cliffs of Rubha na h-Airde Glaise

Coille Iosal and the Braes

Distance 2km **Time** 1 hour
Terrain steep and muddy path, track,
minor road **Map** OS Explorer 410
Access limited bus service (59) from
Portree stops at Braes village hall

A climb though Coille Iosal (Gaelic for
Low Wood) begins this short walk which
has good views over to Raasay and the
Crowlin Islands on a clear day. It is
situated in the Braes, a lovely, fertile
and quiet part of the island, a few miles
south of Portree. The walk can be
combined with the An Aird route to
complete the day.

Start at the Braes village hall where
there is car parking by the recycling bins.
Take the path on the other side of the road
which skirts along the edge of the field
and then heads uphill through woodland
of rowan, birch, oak and hazel. Follow the
small white arrow markers as the path
emerges from the woodland and keeps to
the right of a burn with a cascading series
of small waterfalls.

The faint path now climbs the more
open moorland, crossing a small wooden
bridge up some steps. Continue alongside
an attractive waterfall and rise above it to
a gate. Go though the gate and turn right.

The route now follows a track and passes a seat at a viewpoint with a great outlook over the islands of Raasay, Rona and the Crowlins below. On a clear day you can see the Five Sisters of Kintail ridge on the mainland.

As it continues, the track gives views across the northern part of the Braes and the distinctive small peak of Ben Tianavaig. Pass a small waterworks and electricity substation before emerging on the main Braes road. Here, turn right to return to the village hall.

Before leaving the area, it is worth visiting a small monument about 1km further down the road. In 1882, crofters from here were engaged in a violent struggle when they rebelled against rent increases and evictions across the island. Summonses for the eviction of five men from the community were burnt here, and fearing further unrest 40 policemen were brought in from Glasgow to quell the rebellion and arrest the ringleaders. They detained the men but were ambushed as they headed back to Portree. A volley of stones from the 400 waiting crofters rained down, and the

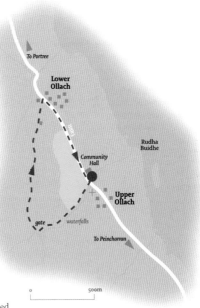

To Portree

Lower Ollach

Rudha Buidhe

Community Hall

Upper Ollach

gate   waterfalls

To Peinchorran

0   500m

policemen fought back with truncheons. Many women both gave and received blows, seven of them being seriously injured by the officers. The ensuing public outcry helped turn the tide against the landowners until a Royal Commission was set up to investigate the crofters' grievances. It was the beginning of the end of the Highland Clearances.

◀ Looking to Ben Tianavaig

An Aird Peninsula

Distance 3km **Time** 1 hour 30
Terrain path to the beach; beyond this it
can be wet **Map** OS Explorer 410 **Access**
limited bus service (59) from Portree
passes Balmeanach road, 1km from the
start of the walk

An exploration of a beautiful
promontory off the coast of the Braes,
joined to the rest of the island by a
narrow spit of land known as a tombolo.
This walk offers superb views across the
Sound of Raasay as well as a visit to a
sandy beach and some fascinating
cliff scenery.

When the Braes road forks, take the
turning on the left signed for Balmeanach.

Some 700m further on, there is a red
postbox on the left side of the road; park
just beyond here. Take the path off
towards the coast; the surface has recently
been reconstructed across the once boggy
ground before it descends the steep grass
bank beyond, passing a bench.

The path ends at a pebble beach, with
the An Aird peninsula visible straight
ahead. Continue round the beach, which
has a fine sandy stretch at the far end
– a beautiful and sheltered spot. Beyond,
follow the grassy coastline, keeping to
the left of a tiny loch, and continue
across boggier ground above a low line
of broken cliffs.

The northern end of An Aird is soon

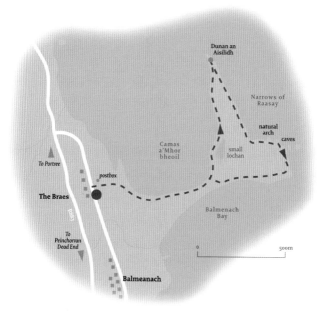

reached, crowned by Dunan an Aisilidh, the site of an ancient fort. Scattered stones are all that remain, but the views – of Ben Tianavaig rising in tiers to the north and of the Isle of Raasay to the east – are magnificent. Seals can often be seen in the straits between here and Raasay; if you are lucky you might catch sight of dolphins or porpoise.

Continue the walk by heading along the seaward coast of the peninsula. This has small but impressive and intricate cliff scenery – it is worth peering down where safe to do so. In early summer there are many nesting razorbills and shags.

The best section is at the far end of the peninsula, where there are at least two natural arches, sea caves and a great blow hole. Take care when exploring near the cliff edges.

Eventually the coast curves back round to the west, with the great cone-shaped peak of Glamaig across the water, to return to the narrow neck of land connecting An Aird with the Braes. Cross this grassy neck to the beach visited earlier, and return by the outward path.

◀ The beach at An Aird

Talisker Bay

Distance 3.5km **Time** 1 hour
Terrain easy track **Map** OS Explorer 410
Access regular bus service (53/54) from
Portree to Carbost, 6km from the start of
the walk

**A striking beach of black and white sand
hemmed in by towering cliffs, Talisker
Bay makes a perfect stroll for a fine
summer's evening.**

From Carbost, take the minor road over
the moors to Talisker. There is limited
parking at the side of the road near the
entrance to Talisker Farm where the road
narrows and divides into three. Follow the
leftmost track through a gate. A short

walk leads to the magnificent
whitewashed Talisker House. Samuel
Johnson and James Boswell stayed here
for a couple of nights during their tour
of the Highlands in 1773; it was the home
of the heir to the Chief of the MacLeods
and 'a better place than one commonly
finds on Skye', according to Boswell.
Johnson sounded less enthusiastic,
finding it 'the place above all that I
have seen from which the gay and jovial
seem utterly excluded, where the hermit
might expect to grow old in meditation,
without possibility of disturbance or
interruption'. The house is now used
for holiday rentals. Keep on the track

◀ The sands of Talisker Bay

with the house on your right and follow the wide valley down towards the sea.

The looming craggy hill of red rock on your left is Preshal More. The energetic Boswell climbed this with the Laird of Coll after dinner whilst the overweight Johnson remained at his writing desk. Their challenging route is now recognised as a scramble and is known as 'Boswell's Buttress'.

The track ends near the sea and an area of large pebbles is crossed to reach the beach over to the right. To the left, the near side of the bay is guarded by a pair of sea stacks, whilst at the far end a stunning waterfall tumbles over the towering cliffs. The sandy beach between has both black and white sand which mix to make beautiful patterns caused by the outgoing tide. This is the most impressive beach on Skye and most walkers will want to linger here before making the return the same way.

A trip to Talisker isn't really complete until you've sampled the famous whisky. The distillery, founded in 1830, is not at Talisker at all but is in the nearby village of Carbost. Today it is a popular visitor attraction, offering tours nicely rounded off with a dram rated as the 'king of drinks' by Robert Louis Stevenson.

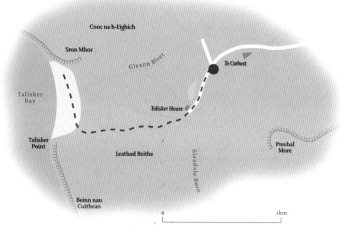

Cnoc na h-Eighich

Sron Mhor

Gleann River

To Carbost

Talisker Bay

Talisker House

Talisker Point

Leathad Beithe

Sleadale Burn

Preshal More

Beinn nan Cuithean

0   1km

The Fairy Pools

Distance **8km** Time **3 hours**
Terrain **rough moorland path, indistinct
and wet in parts** Map **OS Explorer 411**
Access **regular bus service (53/54) from
Portree to Carbost, 7km from the start
of the walk**

**This circuit takes in a series of beautiful
icy clear pools where water cascades
from one to the next and intrepid fairies
may bathe. Beyond the pools, the walk
offers the chance to get close to the
Cuillin without too much ascent. The
return is quieter and has good views
down Glen Brittle.**

The walk starts at the Fairy Pools car
park which is on the right-hand side of
the road as you near the bottom of the
hill heading down into Glen Brittle. Cross
the road from the car park and drop down
the narrow path on the other side. Ignore
a branch path off to your left; this is used
for the return. Cross stepping stones over
a small burn to reach the wider Allt Coir'
a' Mhadaidh further on. This crystal-clear
burn tumbles through an enchanting
series of pools, underwater arches and
circular bowls carved into the rock by the
water. On a hot day, there are some good
spots for a cooling dip.

The obvious path follows the left bank
upstream, passing the pools and crossing
another smaller stream at one point. The
Cuillin Ridge towers ahead, the imposing

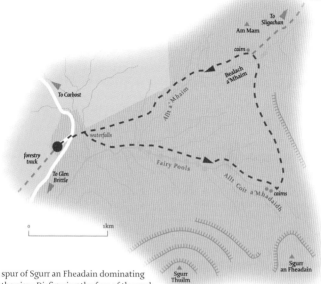

spur of Sgurr an Fheadain dominating the view. Disfiguring the face of the peak is a long dark gash known as Waterpipe Gully. A number of early Victorian climbers tried unsuccessfully to climb the gully, with a successful pair reaching the summit this way in 1895. It still remains a serious challenge, evidenced by the fact that recently a talented group of climbers took seven hours to complete the ascent.

The path becomes stonier and rises fairly steeply as it skirts around the left-hand flank of the base of Sgurr an Fheadain. When the path becomes overrun with stones, look out for a couple of small cairns on the other side of the burn. Once opposite the higher one, make a sharp turn to the left and backtrack on a path heading slightly uphill. The path

back soon becomes clearer as you head away from the water and start to traverse the lower slope of Bruach na Frithe, with the flat ground of Coire na Creiche laid out below. Here the last epic battle between the rival Skye clans – the MacDonalds and the MacLeods – was played out; the name means the Corrie of the Spoils.

Carry on along the narrow path as it crosses the grassy slope and then climbs gently before meeting the path which comes over the Bealach a'Mhaim from Sligachan. Turn left onto this path and follow it as it keeps below the forestry plantation and joins the outward path near the car park.

◀ Sgurr an Fheadain from beside the Allt Coir' a' Mhadaidh

Coire Lagan and the Eas Mor

**Distance 7.5km Time 3 hours 30
Terrain steep paths; optional scree and
scrambling Map OS Explorer 411
Access regular bus service (53/54) from
Portree to Carbost, 12km from Glen Brittle**

This walk takes you into the heart of the
Cuillin, the UK's most alpine mountain
range. Huge cliffs of dark gabbro tower
above, and there are great views out to
the Small Isles of Rum and Canna. The
return path includes the spectacular Eas
Mor waterfall, the highest on Skye.

Start the walk from the parking area at
the end of the road at Glenbrittle Beach.
In the winter the volcanic sand is often
windswept and deserted, whilst in the
summer the popular campsite swells the
number of visitors and the beach can be
a good place for a swim.

Go through the campsite along the
front of the bay, passing to the left of the
small concrete toilet block. Climb the stile
and take the path straight ahead. You will
soon be rising onto the moor and usually
into a breeze, leaving any midges behind.
Cross a track and carry straight on. This
path was a boggy swamp until a few years
ago, but it has now been upgraded into a
fine stone-pitched route. Keep ascending
the moor with the precipices of the
Cuillin becoming ever more dramatic
ahead. Ignore a path off to the right
which crosses a burn and leads into
Coir a'Ghrunnda.

The ascent continues until Loch an
Fhir-bhallaich can be seen over to the
left; watch out for red deer which can
sometimes be seen in this area. Further
on is a large cairn where another path
turns off sharply left – this is the way
back. The Cuillin Ridge can be seen
straight ahead, whilst the vast black
precipice on the right is Sron na Ciche, the

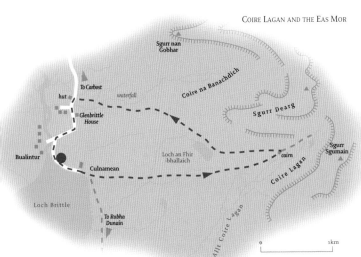

most famous rock-climbing cliff on Skye. Depending on the shadows, you might be able to pick out the giant projecting block of the Cioch, scene of a sword fight in the film *Highlander* and a popular objective for climbers. Out to sea is the jagged outline of the Isle of Rum with the gentler Canna to its right.

For the adventurous it is possible to continue to the small lochan in upper Coire Lagan from this point, which adds a very rugged extra hour to the route. If doing this, carry straight on: the path soon becomes stony and scree covered, but is marked by small cairns in places. As you approach the slabs which descend from the upper corrie, the easiest route is to ascend a small rocky gully up between the slabs. This is a straightforward rocky staircase, though you may need to use your hands at one point. From the top of the gully make a mental note for your return route and continue over the scree and finally some easy-angled gabbro slabs with their incredibly rough non-slip surface to reach the beautiful small lochan encircled by towering peaks and great curtains of scree.

Return to the large cairn on the outward path and this time keep right to follow the recently improved path above Loch an Fhir-bhallaich and down alongside the burn. This soon enters a gorge at an impressive waterfall, the Eas Mor. The path passes a couple of good viewpoints for the waterfall, which is the highest on Skye. Further on, cross the burn on a wooden bridge and emerge onto the road opposite the Glenbrittle Memorial Hut. Turn left along the road and follow it past the farm back to the parking area at the bay.

◄ Rubha Dunain from Coire Lagan

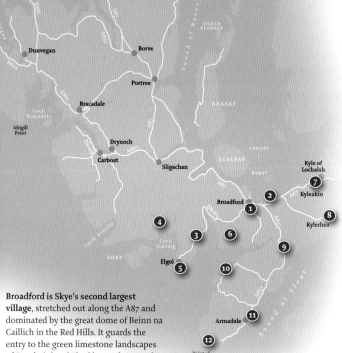

Broadford is Skye's second largest village, stretched out along the A87 and dominated by the great dome of Beinn na Caillich in the Red Hills. It guards the entry to the green limestone landscapes of Strathaird and Elgol beyond. Around Loch Slappin there are wonderful views of Bla Bheinn – reckoned by many to be the most beautiful mountain on Skye – but even these are surpassed by the classic view of the Cuillin across the waters of Loch Scavaig from Elgol.

South of Broadford are the gateways to Skye; Kyleakin, home to the elegant arch of the Skye Bridge and the ruins of Caisteal Maol, and tiny Kylerhea to which the old 'Glenachulish' car ferry still crosses the straits from the mainland during the summer months, giving the most scenic way onto the island.

The landscape changes completely on the Sleat peninsula, which is where the ferry from Mallaig lands. Sheltered from the worst of the winter storms, Sleat is a fertile landscape with many woodlands and has become known as the Garden of Skye. Though it has fewer hills, it looks out onto high mountains on all sides, with the peaks of Knoydart the dominating feature of the landscape.

Broadford and Southern Skye

1 **Skye Marble Line**   58
Follow the old railway which once carried quarried marble from Kilchrist to the pier at Broadford

2 **Rubha Ardnish**   60
This headland is a popular spot for birdwatchers, but remember to keep an eye on the tide as well

3 **Dun Ringill**   62
Fans of cerebral rockers Jethro Tull especially won't want to miss this easy walk to a historic viewpoint

4 **Loch Coruisk**   64
Make sure you don't miss the boat for this trip to some of the very best mountain scenery in Europe

5 **Prince Charlie's Cave**   66
Good scrambling skills are required to visit this hidden cave which is only accessible at low tide

6 **The Clearance Villages**   68
Enjoy great mountain and coastal views as you journey past the silent ruins of old crofting communities

7 **Kyleakin and Caisteal Maol**   70
Keep a look out for passing wildlife while you explore 'Saucy Mary's' castle and the village of Kyleakin

8 **Kylerhea Otter Haven**   72
Patience will have its reward on this leisurely walk to one of the best spots on the island for otter-spotting

9 **Kinloch Forest and Leitir Fura**   74
A wonderful woodland walk to discover an abandoned village overlooking the Sound of Sleat

10 **Dun Scaith Castle**   76
From Tokavaig, explore a quiet stretch of coast and view the ruins of a castle steeped in legend

11 **Armadale Woods**   78
Whether you are a walker or a gardener, you will find inspiration around the grounds of Armadale Castle

12 **The Point of Sleat**   80
Grand views of the Small Isles, Ardnamurchan and Knoydart are the reward for this trek to Skye's most southerly point

Skye Marble Line

Distance **10km** Time **2 hours 30**
Terrain **excellent path** Map **OS Explorer**
412 Access **Broadford is served by regular**
buses from Portree and Kyle of Lochalsh

This walk follows a path along the route
of an old railway; it has been much
upgraded and is one of the few routes on
Skye suitable for some buggies and
wheelchairs. There are good views of the
Red Hills and Bla Bheinn and the route
visits the old marble quarries which have
lain silent for almost a hundred years.

From the large car park in central
Broadford, walk along the main road west
until you reach the bridge over the
Broadford River. Just before the bridge,
turn left onto a signed path that runs

between the river and the Broadford Hotel.
This waterside path soon takes you to the
Elgol road. Turn right along the road and
climb gently uphill, passing a plantation.
Beyond this, take a signposted turn to the
left onto an all-terrain footpath.

You are now walking on the remains of
the railway that carried marble from the
mines at Kilchrist to the pier at Broadford.
Marble was mined at the end of this track
from the early 18th century until the last
mine closed in 1912. It is believed that an
aerial rope-way was initially used to
transport the marble and that this was
replaced by a small locomotive when the
railway line was built. Marble is still
quarried at nearby Torrin and its gravel
and chippings are used for local

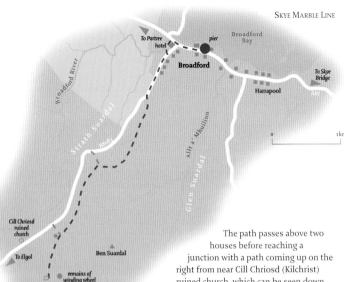

To Portree
hotel

pier

Broadford Bay

Broadford

To Skye
Bridge

Harrapool

A87

Broadford River

Strath Suardal

B8083

Allt a' Mhuilinn

Glen Suardal

0   1km

Cill Chriosd
ruined
church

To Elgol

Ben Suardal

remains of
winding wheel

path to
coast

driveways; up until the 1970s many of the island's roads were chipped with the distinctive white marble that shone brightly in the sun on fine days.

Carry on along the course of the old railway as it contours the hillside and passes through two small gates. Ignore the turning to the right and continue up the path as it crests a rise to reveal a view of green Strath Suardal ahead. Even today, you can see that the underlying limestone has enabled lush grass to grow high on the hillsides here, making this glen one of the most fertile and populated on the island before the Clearances.

The path passes above two houses before reaching a junction with a path coming up on the right from near Cill Chriosd (Kilchrist) ruined church, which can be seen down by the road: continue straight ahead on the main path.

Soon the small heaps of waste marble from the lower mine are reached. The surfaced path ends here, but it is worth continuing on the rockier track ahead, climbing more steeply for the last section to the higher mine. Here, the circular remains of a winding wheel can be seen. This was used to pull the railway wagons up the steep incline. You can explore the remains of the quarry workings and enjoy the views across to the great peak of Bla Bheinn on a fine day. Return by the outward route; if time allows you can take a signed 1.5km detour to see the remains of the church and churchyard of Cill Chriosd by turning left from the Marble Line.

◄ Remains of railway winding wheel with the Broadford Red Hills behind

Rubha Ardnish

Distance 6.5km **Time** 2 hours 30
Terrain grassy foreshore, no path, boggy
but level **Map** OS Explorer 412
Access regular bus services between
Broadford and Kyle of Lochalsh; get off
at Waterloo

**One of the best walks on Skye for keen
birdwatchers, the low-lying Ardnish
peninsula makes for a tranquil escape
from the bustle of Broadford. At the end
is a tiny island accessible only when
the tide is low.**

Start the walk at the beginning of the
Waterloo road from Broadford. There is a
lay-by on the seaward side of the main
road a few metres north towards
Broadford. Follow the Waterloo road as it
skirts the coast, passing the varied houses
and crofts. For many years the Army
provided one of the few sources of
employment on Skye, and this area was
settled by soldiers returning from the
Battle of Waterloo in 1815. There are
excellent views back over Broadford and
to Beinn Caillich behind. At low tide, this
is a favoured spot for local winkle and
whelk collectors, although they have to
compete with the seagulls.

Just past the final house, a small gate
leads through to the start of the grassy
peninsula leading to Ardnish Point.
The gravelled path to the right leads to
Breakish. Ignore this route and instead
turn left down to the shore. From here,
follow the shore all the way to the
headland. At times there are faint paths
through the grass but, depending on the

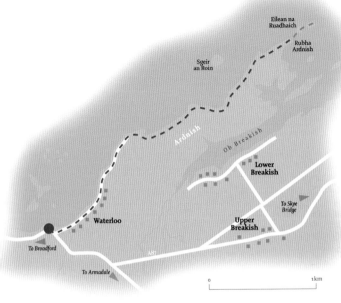

state of the tide, you can walk anywhere as long as you keep the sea on your left. After a while, you cross a large basalt dyke running out into the sea. At low tide you can see a criss-cross pattern of these dykes sticking up above the softer rock. Seals can often be spotted either swimming in the water or basking like fat bananas on semi-submerged rocks.

Once you reach the point, you can explore the tiny islet of Eilean na Ruadhaich if the tide allows. This beautiful spot has stretches of bright white coral sand and anemone-filled rockpools. It is also a great viewpoint across the Inner Sound to Applecross and

the Skye Bridge at Kyle of Lochalsh. Just remember not to be caught out by the tide which quickly fills the channel between this small island and the rest of Ardnish.

Return by the same route or the slightly higher ground just inland if you want a change from the foreshore. This part of Skye is a birdwatchers' mecca, with enthusiasts recording vast numbers of plover, oystercatchers, purple sandpipers, turnstones, lapwings and snipe. It is also a good place to watch for otters: evidence of their activity is shown by the bright green grassy mounds fertilised by white splashes of otter spraint.

◀ Low tide at Rubha Ardnish

Dun Ringill

Distance 3km **Time** 1 hour 30
Terrain grassy paths, boggy in places
Map OS Explorer 412 **Access** take the Elgol
bus from Broadford (49) and get off at
Kirkibost, a short distance from the start
of the walk

This short coastal and woodland walk
visits two crumbling historical sites.
The Kilmarie Chambered Cairn is one
of the largest on the island, but non-
archaeologists are likely to be more
intrigued by Dun Ringill – once an
Iron Age broch, in medieval times a clan
stronghold and today a peaceful eyrie
perched above the sea.

Take the minor road which branches off
the Broadford to Elgol road at Kirkibost
and heads down to Kilmarie. There is a
small parking area beyond the house
where the road reaches the shore. Until
1994, Kilmarie House was the home of Ian
Anderson, singer and flautist of the rock
group Jethro Tull. When he left he sold
the main part of his estate – most of
Strathaird – to the John Muir Trust who
now manage the area with conservation
as a priority. Head back along the road
until a small metal gate on the right
marks the start of a footpath into the
woods. take this path, crossing an ornate
iron footbridge over the stream. On the
far side, follow the path on the right along
a grassy shelf above the water. Soon it
leads out of the woods to the bay beyond,
passing some stepping stones that lead
back to the parking area. Pass but do not
go through a gate on the left; instead keep
to the grass along the outside of a fence.
When the fence turns left, carry straight
on across a burn to reach a stile in the
next section of fence. Cross this and
follow a boggy section of path that heads
diagonally uphill.

Soon the path joins a larger one coming
in from the left – this route is used for the

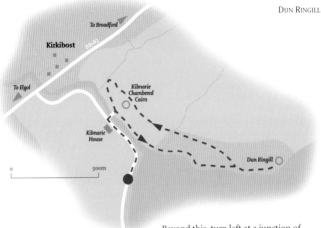

return. Continue straight on as the path crosses open ground set back slightly from the coast. After passing a sea inlet with sculpted rocks, the remains of Dun Ringill come into view ahead, a tumbledown ruin on a crag above the sea. The entrance is intact and it is possible to crawl through into what must have once been the keep, but only a couple of sections of wall remain. Nonetheless, this is an atmospheric spot, and it inspired Jethro Tull's Anderson to write the hit song *Dun Ringill*. It was the original seat of the MacKinnon clan (who later moved to Caisteal Maol at Kyleakin), but there had been a defensive building on this site for many centuries before that.

Return to the path junction reached earlier. This time, continue ahead along the main path; this soon reaches the woods and crosses a small burn. Bear right uphill here; there is a grassy path through the trees, soon passing a bench.

Beyond this, turn left at a junction of paths. The walk now passes some stone ruins, backed by a view of the twin summits of Bla Bheinn. Turn left at yet another fork, beyond which the path soon becomes a track. When the track slopes downhill, look out for a path that leads down through the woods to the left – the start is marked by a 'No Camping, No Fires' sign. This takes you back to the footbridge near the start of the walk.

Immediately before reaching the bridge, the Kilmarie Chambered Cairn can be seen on the left. It may look like an overgrown grassy mound, but it is regarded as one of the best examples of these structures on the island. At the top of the cairn is a small cist or stone chamber; this was used for a burial. A beaker found in this cist can now be seen in the National Museum of Scotland in Edinburgh. The cairn is fragile so take great care not to damage it before returning over the bridge to the start.

◄ Remains of Dun Ringill

Loch Coruisk

Distance 7km **Time** 3 hours 30
Terrain very boggy, rough path, river
crossings **Map** OS Explorer 411
Access regular bus service (49) from
Broadford to Elgol, boat to Loch Coruisk

**A fantastic walk in the very heart of the
Cuillin without any need to scale the
heights. If the circuit is too much, it is
still well worth doing the first section for
the awe-inspiring surroundings.**

From Elgol there are two operators
running trips to Loch Coruisk, an amazing
expanse of water encircled by the high
cliffs and crags of the Black Cuillin. These
trips usually need to be booked in advance
by phone and you should make sure the
timetables will leave you enough time to
complete the walk between their morning
trip (for your outward journey) and the
late afternoon return trip to bring you
back. It can usually be done
between the boat times
comfortably, but keep an

eye on the clock and turn back if you are in
any doubt as to whether you will make it.

The boat trip itself has wonderful views as
the Cuillin are gradually approached across
Loch Scavaig, a wide sea loch. Seals are
usually seen from the boat, and frequently
porpoise or even otters or dolphins can be
sighted. You may go close to the 'bad-step',
a rocky obstacle that has to be crossed by
walkers making the long trek to Coruisk
from Elgol or Camasunary on foot – one slip
here and they end up in the water below.
The boat then moors at a landing stage in
Loch na Cuilce, the bay of Loch Scavaig, in
the shadow of the mountains.

Begin the walk by ascending the roughly
constructed steps which lead inland.
The Scavaig – one of the shortest rivers in
Scotland – cascades into the sea over rock
slabs to your right, whilst further out to
sea can be seen the bold outline of the Isle
of Rum and neighbouring Eigg. Continue
near the river almost to where it issues
from Loch Coruisk. Here turn right and
cross the river using the piled stones – this

can usually be done with dry feet but may be impossible after heavy rain.

The path then climbs a short distance to give a magnificent full-length view of Loch Coruisk. Follow the path a little way before heading back down and keeping to the shore; the higher path climbs over the pass towards Glen Sligachan. Soon you will reach the Allt a'Choire Riabhach. This is most easily crossed where it runs across the flat section close to the loch shore; again avoid the path climbing up the east bank which leads towards Glen Sligachan.

After crossing a pebbly beach, the slopes of the Druim nam Ramh now begin to close in on the right and the route keeps beside the loch. At one point, the path passes through an area littered with giant grey boulders; these came down in a rockfall around ten years ago, though the colourings make them look much more recent. Continue by the shore; there are a couple of rocky sections to negotiate as well as the bogs.

Pass an area of rowan trees before reaching the head of the loch. Cross the water flowing into it just before a large rocky outcrop topped with a prominent boulder. From here, there are fantastic views of the main summits on the Cuillin Ridge above the upper Coir-uisg basin. With binoculars you may be able to make

out climbers and scramblers on different routes. The great peak that dominates the west side of Coruisk – with a huge ridge descending almost to the loch – is Sgurr Dubh Mor. The ridge is the Dubhs Ridge, one of Britain's longest rock climbs.

Cross the burn and continue back down the far side of the loch. There are areas of flat slabs that make for easier walking, giving some relief from the bogs. The dark rocks around Coruisk (and through most of the Cuillin) are Gabbro – a volcanic rock with a remarkably rough surface, perfect for climbers. Eventually, the end of the loch is reached and the path down to the waiting boat for the return to Elgol – if you've got your timings right.

Prince Charlie's Cave

Distance 4km **Time** 2 hours 30
Terrain very boggy paths, optional rock
scramble to cave **Map** OS Explorer 411
Access regular bus service (49) from
Broadford to Elgol

Following his flight across the island,
Bonnie Prince Charlie ate his last meal
and spent his final night on Skye in a
hidden cave at the tip of the Strathaird
peninsula. Entering the cave requires
some scrambling and is only possible
for an hour or so each side of low tide
(check timetables locally), but the walk
to it has some of the best coastal views
in Scotland.

There is parking at the jetty in Elgol, but
in high season it is usually full.
Alternative parking is back up the hill
near the teashop, or by the community
centre 50m along the Glasnakillie road.
Save this walk for a clear day as Elgol is
famed for its view of the Cuillin.

Begin from the top level of parking
above the jetty, where a stony slope leads
to a rough path rising up across the moor
to the right.

The path runs mostly along the edge of
the cliffs, set back slightly from the sea;
the going is very boggy in one or two
places and the way not always clear. The
compensation is in the views – looking
back, majestic Bla Bheinn has joined the
rest of the Cuillin, whilst ahead is the
dramatic outline of the Isle of Rum, with
Canna to its right. After little over 1km,
you reach a grassy neck of land that
connects the headland of Suidhe nan Eun
to the rest of the coast. Wander down
onto this narrow neck for a view of a
broad sea stack before returning to
continue along the cliffs. The Cuillin are
now left behind but the Isle of Eigg
appears as compensation, identifiable by
a prominent dip in its middle.

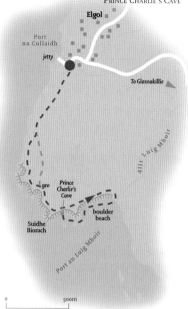

A geo – a deep sea inlet – breaks into the coastline a little further on: detour round this to the left to continue the walk. Beyond is the overhanging grassy top of Suidhe Biorach (Gaelic for the Pointed Seat): according to local folklore childless women who sit atop this crag will bear children. The cliffs fall away at the wide Port an Luig Mhoir bay. Go down to the shore here, aiming right along the base of the cliff to reach a beach of boulders. If you checked the tides and arrived here shortly before low tide, you should have time to try to find and explore the cave. Reaching it involves a rock-scramble, and even getting to the foot of this means crossing awkward boulders, so if unsure it is best to omit this part of the walk. Otherwise, head carefully along the boulder shore to the right, towards Suidhe Biorach.

At the obvious dark cleft in the cliffs, a first cave is reached. This is a through cave, submerged by the sea for most of the day; continue beyond this, passing its second entrance leading back under the cliff. Prince Charlie's cave is completely hidden from beach level, the entrance being above the high tide mark and the tumble of boulders choking the bottom of the very next cleft in the cliffs. These boulders can be climbed by the agile – taking great care – there are some footholds on the rock-wall to the left. Above this awkward

obstacle, the ground descends slightly into the wide cave entrance where Prince Charlie had his farewell feast. He had landed in the Trotternish peninsula six days previously, having been famously rowed to Skye in company of Flora MacDonald. To reach Elgol he had to march by night from Portree.

Take care to keep an eye on the tides to ensure you don't become trapped. Carefully make the descent back down to the beach and return to the clifftop path. Follow this back to Elgol the same way; you can cut across the corner from the deep geo passed on the walk out.

◀ Suidhe Biorach cliffs near Prince Charlie's cave

67

The Clearance Villages

Distance **17km** Time **6 hours**
Terrain **paths, tracks, minor road**
Map **OS Explorer 412** Access **regular bus
service (49) from Broadford to Elgol; get
off at Kilchrist ruined church**

**Retrace the route taken by the villagers of
Boreraig and Suisnish when they were
forcibly cleared from their homes in 1852.
Now deserted, the picturesque ruins
provide a tranquil day-long walk with
lovely coastal and mountain views.**

Start at the ruined church of Kilchrist,
6km southwest of Broadford on the Elgol
road. The atmospheric ruin dates from the
16th century when this was the heart of
one of Skye's most fertile and populous
districts. Walk along the road towards
Broadford for a short distance until you
reach a track going off to the right. This
reaches the remains of the old marble
factory; keep left of this on a rough track
up the moor.

This track reaches a well-maintained
path which is the route of the old railway

used to move marble from the quarries
here to the quay at Broadford. The quarries
closed in 1912 (there is still one left at
Torrin); turn right and follow the route
through a gate to pass the spoil heaps and
remains of buildings.

At the upper quarry, the path divides
with a branch heading downhill to the
right; continue ascending the main path.
After passing a cairn at the summit of the
pass, with great views back towards the
dramatic mountain of Bla Bheinn, the
track narrows to become a path and goes
through a gate. The fenced area is part of
the Beinn nan Carn Native Woodland
project, where native trees have been
planted and regeneration is being
encouraged. The path follows a burn on
the left and then climbs slightly before
descending to the coast.

Pass to the right of some sheepfolds and
continue down to the shore as the path
becomes indistinct amongst old green
fields and ruined houses. This is Boreraig, a
fertile, sheltered and beautiful spot. It was

◄ Remains of a house at Boreraig

brutally cleared by Lord MacDonald, all residents being evicted and their homes burned to make way for the more profitable sheep. There were 12 drystone-built houses and 15 outbuildings here, and it is possible to imagine the community as it once was.

From Boreraig, follow a coastal path to the right after crossing a burn on the stone slab bridge just above the shore. The path passes to the left of the last building in Boreraig, keeping directly on the shoreline where the cliffs press close. This was once the main route to Boreraig for the villagers and, as a result of being built and graded well, it remains an easy path to follow. However, in a couple of places slippages from the cliffs have caused the route to weave between fallen rocks. After wet weather, there are high waterfalls cascading down the black cliffs in two or three places along this section. The path then climbs and continues at a higher level until the remains of the settlement of Suisnish come into view. Ahead is a large fenced field with a barn on the far side. When you reach the fence, follow the path on the outside of the fence to the right and around the corner of the field. Pass through the gate on the left and descend to the barn below. Go through another gate to the right of the barn where a good

landrover track begins, taking you past the less well preserved remains of Suisnish.

The track passes a shepherd's house that was occupied until the late 1950s and still retains its roof and some fittings, leading you northwards for 3km until the pebble beach at Camas Malag is reached. There are fantastic views across Loch Slappin to the southern end of the Cuillin and the Red Hills. At Camas Malag bay follow the road uphill away from the coast, with views of the Torrin Marble Quarry. Soon the junction with the Broadford to Elgol road is reached. Turn right here and follow the road back to the start, passing picturesque Loch Cill Chriosd on the way.

Kyleakin and Caisteal Maol

Distance 3.5km Time 1 hour 30
Terrain coastal path, minor roads
Map OS Explorer 412 Access regular bus
service (50/55) from Portree and
Broadford to Kyleakin

**An interesting exploration of the village
of Kyleakin, taking in a ruined castle with
good views over the straits to Kyle of
Lochalsh and a closer look at the elegant
Skye Bridge.**

Kyleakin was once the busy gateway to
Skye, where the ferry arrived over the
narrow straits from Kyle of Lochalsh and
there were often long queues of traffic.
With the opening of the bridge in 1995,
the village became a quiet backwater and
headquarters for the regular protests
against the bridge tolls which, until they
were abolished in December 2004, made

the bridge the most expensive stretch of
road in the world.

Start the route from the large car park
opposite the village green. Walk along the
road past the King Haakon's Bar; a path to
the left offers a short detour up to the
village war memorial which offers
excellent views. Returning to the road,
make a detour to the harbourside to see
the bronze otter by renowned local
sculptor Lawrence Broderick, with a view
over to Caisteal Maol. The walk continues
by a path opposite the war memorial
path, heading to the right along the
water's edge to cross the bridge over the
river to South Obbe, Kyleakin's hidden
corner. Turn left along the road until it
ends at a pier and then follow the path
which leads around the coast towards
Caisteal Maol. It emerges onto the beach
at a large boathouse. The route continues

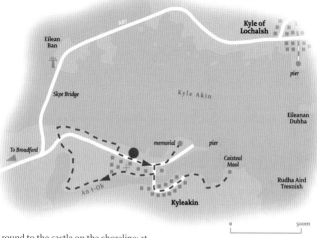

round to the castle on the shoreline; at low tide this is simple enough but at high tide some very rough detours inland may be necessary. A steep path climbs up to the castle, passing a bench.

Caisteal Maol (often anglicised to Castle Moil) is situated in the perfect lookout spot with commanding views over the narrow waters in both directions. There has been a fortress on this site since the 10th century. According to legend it was built by 'Saucy Mary', a Norse princess who married into the local MacKinnon clan. The MacKinnons made a living by exacting a toll from ships passing through the straits. After exploring the small ruins, return to the bridge from South Obbe by the same path.

Cross the bridge and this time turn immediately left onto a grassy path. This leads into an area of tidal salt marsh which is blanketed by pink thrift flowers

in summer. Follow the path as it curves to the right, passing the pond which is the source of the river and heading between the village hall and primary school to emerge on the main road.

Cross the road and take a narrow path towards the water straight ahead, soon reaching a telescope and some benches. From here, there is a good view of the Skye Bridge and Eilean Ban, the White Island, with its lighthouse now dwarfed by the modern bridge. The cottage visible on the island was the last home of the famous wildlife writer Gavin Maxwell, author of *Ring of Bright Water*. The island and cottage can be visited via a boat trip from the Bright Water Visitor Centre. Just above the beach, turn right onto a path and follow the coast back towards the village centre, passing a community garden and wildlife hide.

◀ Kyleakin Lighthouse on Eilean Ban under the Skye Bridge

Kylerhea Otter Haven

Distance 2.5km **Time** 1 hour **Terrain easy
level track, optional loop with flights of
wooden steps** Map OS Explorer 412
Access regular bus service (50/55) from
Broadford to Kyleakin; limited service
(61) to Glenelg from Shiel Bridge

**This easy walk has great views over the
narrow straits to the mainland and the
chance to watch for otters from the hide.
The start can be reached either by taking
the tiny and original Skye ferry from
Glenelg or by tackling the dramatic
mountain road from Broadford that
plunges steeply down to Kylerhea.**

Turn up a track signed for Kylerhea
Otter Haven, off to the left as you come
down the hill towards the ferry. At the
parking area, there are picnic tables with
fabulous views over the water below to
the pretty bay at Glenelg and to the
mountains beyond. The walk begins
along the track from the parking area.
It soon passes a toilet block and
continues through attractive mixed
woodland. Felling at regular intervals
allows good views of the water below,
where you should see the old
'Glenachulish' ferry crossing to and fro
with its cargo of just four cars. There are
also a number of wooden benches to
encourage you to take the walk at a
leisurely pace.

When you reach a fork, turn right down
a path that leads to the otter hide. This
wooden building has an excellent view
over the shoreline below. Seals and a large
variety of birds can usually be seen from

the hide; otters are more elusive and much patience is required. During the summer months, a warden can give you tips on spotting them. Look for the tell-tale 'V' shape in the water, and keep them in sight with your binoculars. Once they come ashore they are easily lost in the camouflage of the kelp and rocks. The hide is open all year, but only manned and supplied with binoculars during the summer months. The whole of the Skye coastline is one of the best places in Britain to see otters and the information provided at the Otter Haven is a good way to start your search.

Kylerhea is close to three of the former homes of the writer Gavin Maxwell; to the south, just beyond Glenelg is Sandaig, imortalised as Camusfearna in his book *Ring of Bright Water*. Here he lived with a succession of otters until a series of incidents of bad luck prompted a move, first to Isle Ornsay, and finally to Eilean Ban, the tiny island between Kyle of Lochalsh and Kyleakin that is now crossed by the Skye Bridge. Here the Bright Water

Trust has restored his house and built an otter hide that is open to visitors by arrangement; ask at the Bright Water Visitor Centre in Kyleakin.

Leaving the hide, take the path to the right and accompany it through the woods to a small wooden bridge. The path turns back on itself and climbs two flights of steps before emerging on a forestry track. Turn left and follow this back to the parking area.

◂ The Kyle Rhea narrows from the Otter Haven hide

Kinloch Forest and Leitir Fura

Distance 6.5km Time 3 hours
Terrain clear path, steep in places
Map OS Explorer 412 Access regular bus
service (51/52) from Broadford and
Portree to Armadale passes the end of
the Kinloch Forest road

This circuit passes through beautiful
woodland to visit the remains of the
deserted village of Leitir Fura. The village
overlooks the Sound of Sleat, with
stunning views across the water to
Knoydart and the great peak of Beinn
Sgritheall with the tiny islands of
Sandaig below.

The starting point for this walk is
the Kinloch Forest car park which is

reached from the A851, 6km south of
Skulamus. At the car park, there is a
part-reconstructed blackhouse and
information boards about the wildlife
and history of the area. Follow the main
track uphill from the car park. The white
buildings of Kinloch Lodge are visible
below through gaps in the trees: this is
the present home of the MacDonald clan
chief, where chef Lady Claire MacDonald
runs her famed cookery courses.

After passing through a gate, take the
waymarked path which rises up through
the woods to the left. There are wonderful
views back to Isle Ornsay, and, as the walk
progresses, even better vistas of Knoydart,
Loch Huorn and the Sandaig Islands just

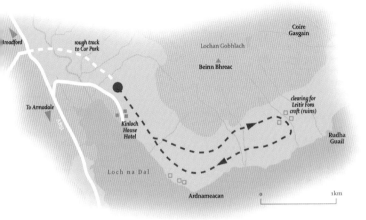

off the mainland ahead. Ignore the first turning off to the right and continue along the main path. Further on, follow the main path downhill to the right, ignoring the smaller path ahead which is the old drover's path through to Kylerhea.

The path winds downhill to Leitir Fura, the site of a small village abandoned early in the 19th century when most of the inhabitants left for a new life in Nova Scotia. The villagers were woodkeepers for the MacDonalds who sold the valuable oak trunks for boat building and the oak and birch bark to the leather tanning industry. Life was made harder by a ban on taking any of the surrounding wood for their own use, and one family was evicted in punish-ment for their children accidentally setting fire to the large oak tree, the Fura Mor, which gave the village its name. More recently, descendants of the original inhabitants visited from Canada and planted a new oak tree. The area is now part of the Millennium Forest for Scotland which aims to restore native woodlands.

Follow the twisting path through the remains of the houses before it reaches the main forestry track below. Turn right here to return to the car park, with good views over the Kylerhea narrows all the way. On the final approach to the start, there are unexpected distant glimpses of the Cuillin Ridge, Bla Bheinn and the Red Hills ahead.

◄ Looking across to Knoydart from Leitir Fura

75

Dun Scaith Castle

Distance 1.5km Time 40 mins
Terrain **straightforward walk on tracks
and then a grassy path, fairly level**
Map **OS Explorer 412** Access **no regular
bus service to Tokavaig; bus (51/52) from
Broadford to Armadale, 12km away**

A short, level walk to the ruins of Dun
Scaith Castle which has an intriguing
past. It has a spectacular coastal location
with fantastic views across the sea loch
to the Cuillin.

The walk starts from the eastern end of
the bay at Tokavaig, Ob Gauscavaig, just
before the road starts to rise steeply.
There is parking at the roadside opposite
the bay. Walk along the road away from
the two houses until a cattle grid is
crossed and a track branches off to the
left. Take this track and follow it across
the head of the bay towards a house and
derelict outbuilding, where it becomes

grassier. Keep to the left of the house,
following a grassy path out to the remains
of Dun Scaith Castle.

The castle, which occupies the site of a
much earlier vitrified fort, is perched on
an offshore rock. The 6m-wide gully was
bridged by two walls which flanked a
drawbridge. The pivot holes are still
visible on the far side – a door would have
opened onto a flight of stone steps
enclosed by two walls which led into the
courtyard of the castle. The remains of a
well and a large tower have also been
found. The drawbridge has long since
gone and the walls themselves are
crumbling making access to the castle
itself extremely dangerous. At low tide,
it is possible to scramble around the
seaward side of the castle and view the
remains of the curtain wall – one of the
earliest surviving examples of lime-
mortared construction found on Skye.

76

◂ Bla Bheinn seen from near Dun Scaith

The castle was a stronghold of the MacLeod of MacLeod, now of Dunvegan Castle, before it became the principal seat of the MacDonalds of Skye in the 15th century. Among the many legends associated with Dun Scaith are those recounted in Macpherson's *Ossian* concerning the adventures of the Irish folk hero Cu Chulainn, who came here when he first landed in Skye. One tradition tells how he came to learn the martial arts of war from the warrior queen 'Sgathaich', whose home this was at that time.

From the low cliffs just to the right of the castle are fantastic views over Loch Eishort to the Cuillin mountains. Directly opposite are the remains of the cleared villages of Suisnish and Boreraig. When you have finished admiring the view and exploring the coast, the return route is by the same path past the old house and along the track back to the road at Tokavaig.

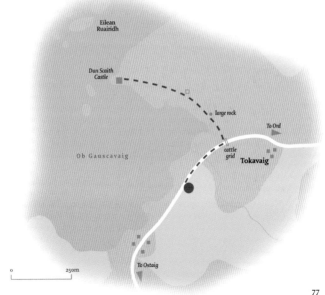

77

Armadale Woods

Distance 5.5km **Time** 2 hours
Terrain paths, tracks Map OS Explorer 412
Access regular bus service (51/52) from
Portree and Broadford to Armadale

The gardens surrounding the ruins of
Armadale Castle are one of Skye's most
popular attractions. This walk explores
the nature trails that have been set up
through the surrounding woods and
hills; on a clear day, the views across to
the mainland are superb.

From the visitor centre at Armadale
Castle, walk past the stable block and café
along the A851 towards Armadale Pier for
a short distance. Take the first tarmac
road on the right which heads uphill,
ignoring the signposted path to the pier,
then take the next left which is signed for
Armadale Hill. This road climbs steeply to
a row of holiday chalets. Here, keep right
onto a track through a gateway and follow
it as it skirts the edge of the woodland.

The track climbs and heads into the
woods, passing over a wooden bridge

and to the right of a derelict cottage.
It narrows to become a path, crossing a
vehicle track. Turn left at a signposted
fork, still following the signs for
Armadale Hill. From here, the path rises
through the trees and there are fabulous
views back across the water to Knoydart.
Keep left at another fork to continue
climbing and eventually emerge into an
open area of bracken and grass.

Another signed junction is reached.
Turn left and follow the track through a
plantation to reach a large gate leading
onto open moorland. Keep straight ahead
on the track, which can be muddy, and
cross the open moorland. When you are
alongside the small dome of Armadale
Hill, which has a wooden post on the
summit, turn right and climb up a faint
grassy path to the top. On a clear day there
are fantastic views across the water to
Mallaig and Knoydart, with the mountains
of Ladhar Bheinn and Beinn Sgritheall
prominent, as well as down onto the
Armadale Woods. However, as Knoydart

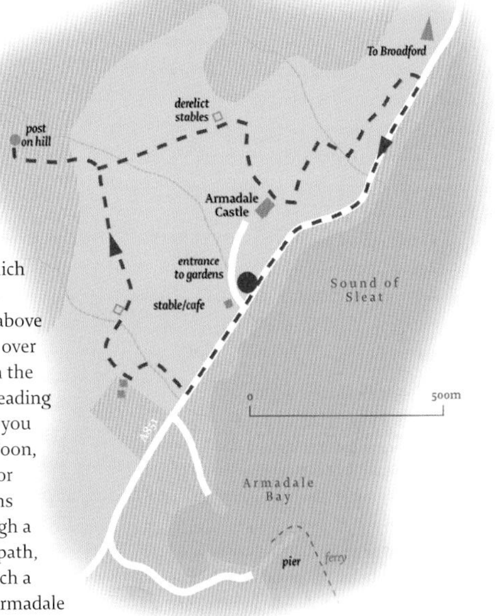

◀ Armadale Castle

has a reputation as Britain's wettest place, don't be surprised if it's shrouded in cloud.

Retrace your steps back to the last junction in the woods. This time take the left turn, which is signed for The Steading, and follow the path as it descends above a grazing field. There are views over the ruins of the castle and then the track passes to the right of a steading where you turn right, heading downhill. Soon, take a path on the left signed for the Red Trail and Castle Gardens and then left again. Pass through a gate and follow the woodland path, eventually heading right to reach a white building at the back of Armadale Castle. From here, you can either continue on the Red Trail as described here or turn right and explore the castle gardens for which an entrance fee is payable.

Armadale was home to the MacDonald chiefs on and off from the 15th century until 1925 when the present house, which had been extensively damaged by fire in 1855, was left to the wind and rain and became the ruin you see today. Flora MacDonald, who helped Bonnie Prince Charlie escape to Skye, was married here in 1790. The estate is now run by the Clan Donald Lands Trust who have undertaken restoration work on the gardens and buildings and built the Museum of the

Isles which documents 1500 years of history, culture and bloody battles.

If continuing on the nature trail, keep to the left of the castle and continue alongside the lawn. Turn left, passing a model of a wooden boat, and follow this path, ignoring the first turn on the right but taking a second one. This immediately leads to a T-junction: to the right is a viewpoint over the Sound, but our route turns left through a gate. The path slopes down to the road, where you turn right and cross to join the pathway on the seaward side which makes a pleasant return route to the car park.

Map labels: To Broadford · post on hill · derelict stables · Armadale Castle · entrance to gardens · stable/cafe · Sound of Sleat · Armadale Bay · pier · ferry · 0 500m · A851

The Point of Sleat

Distance 8.5km **Time** 3 hours 30
Terrain rough track and path
Map OS Explorer 412 **Access** no regular
bus service to Aird; bus (51/52) from
Broadford to Armadale, 7km away

**A popular walk to the southernmost
point of Skye, with sweeping sea views to
the Small Isles and Knoydart on the
mainland. The route visits a hidden
sandy cove perfect for a break, whilst the
windswept lighthouse at the point itself
is a good place to spot seabirds and
marine mammals.**

   This walk starts from the very end of the
Sleat road after Aird of Sleat and 7km from
the ferry at Armadale. There is a parking
area just beyond the gallery in the old
church here. Go through the farm gate and
follow the track as it climbs the hillside.
Looking back, the green crofts and white
houses of the settlement of Aird of Sleat
are strung out over the undulating hills.
As the track rises, the mountains of
Knoydart on the mainland can be seen.
Keep to the track as it crosses a stretch of
featureless moorland, often populated
with small herds of grazing cattle.

   After 2.5km, you will start to descend
steeply alongside a pretty burn. Eventually,
a couple of houses come into sight on the
coast ahead. Where the track bends left
just before a fence, take a steep rocky path
left signed Point of Sleat. (This turning
can be hard to spot.) The path crosses a
section of moorland, which can be wet

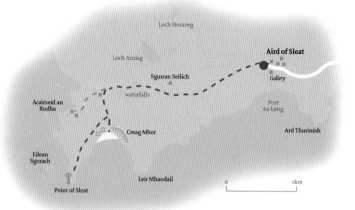

Loch Horaveg

Loch Aruisg

Aird of Sleat

Sgurran Seilich

Gallery

waterfalls

Acairseid an
Rudha

Port
na Long

Creag Mhor

Ard Thurinish

Eilean
Sgorach

Leir Mhaodail

Point of Sleat

0   1km

underfoot, next to a fence and stays close to the fence as it curves right and passes two gates – do not go through either. At the second gate, turn left away from the fence and pass between two low hills.

Here, you can descend to the bay straight ahead or take the right-hand turn up the hill path to continue to the lighthouse. Both paths have waymarker posts, which can be hard to spot in the heather. If detouring to the lovely sandy bay of Camas Daraich, take the path heading downhill towards the sea. Bear right across the slabby rocks on the shore to reach the perfect cove of fine sand. This is a hidden gem of a beach, usually sheltered from the wind and a wonderful spot to relax on a fine summer's day.

To head to the lighthouse, return up the path from the beach to the junction with the marker post. Take the path to the left which climbs up over heather moorland

before reaching a flight of concrete steps. Descend these and follow the faint path around the coast to cross a narrow strip of land with a small bay on either side. There is a small boat landing pier on the left-hand side.

Climb the grassy hillock straight ahead to reach the point itself and the small automatic lighthouse set on the rocks. There has been a lighthouse here since 1938, although the uninspired design of the modern one dates back only to 2003. On a clear day it is obvious that the point is a great location for a lighthouse, with 360-degree views taking in the Cuillin to the north, the distinctive outlines of the isles of Rum and Eigg, and the peninsula of Ardnamurchan to the south. This is a good spot for seeing dolphins and other marine mammals and seabirds such as cormorants and shags. Return the same way.

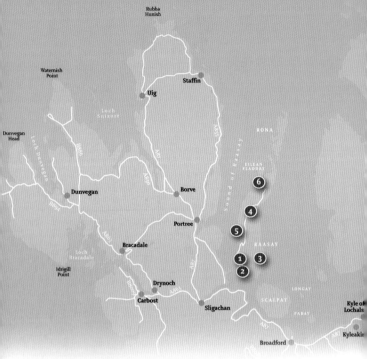

Only a 15-minute ferry ride away from the village of Sconser is the beautiful island of Raasay. Just off Skye's east coast but a world apart, Raasay provides the complete escape from the tourist routes. Whilst Skye is for the most part bare, sweeping and majestic, Raasay offers a more intimate and secretive landscape with woods, bays and hidden glens.

Walkers come here, if at all, to climb the flat-topped volcano of Dun Caan, but for the less ambitious walker there is a fabulous array of old paths. Western Raasay has beautiful bays and woods overlooking Skye, whilst its eastern side has the sad remains of the villages of Hallaig and Screapadal, cleared by a landlord who even banned marriage in his attempts to rid Raasay of its people.

Up the northern end of Raasay is a testament to their desire to stay, where Calum's Road leads to Arnish and is a permanent memorial to the determination of the man who built it with pick and shovel.

The Isle of Raasay

1 **Churchton Bay and Raasay Woods** 84
Enjoy great views of Ben Tianavaig
and the Trotternish Ridge as you
wander on this quiet coastline

2 **The Ironstone Mine and
the Burma Road** 86
Explore Raasay's short-lived industrial
heritage and the remarkable legacy
of its First World War POWs

3 **Hallaig** 88
This beautiful spot with its evocative
ruins is probably the Highlands'
best-known Clearance site

4 **Screapadal and Brochel Castle** 90
The mountains of Applecross
dominate the view as you take in this
old township and ruined castle

5 **Inver Bay and the Sound
of Raasay** 92
Pack a picnic for this remote beach
with a fantastic outlook over the
Sound of Raasay

6 **Calum's Road, Torran and Fladday** 94
A remarkable road leads to the
most isolated part of Raasay and
unforgettable views over to Skye

Churchton Bay and Raasay Woods

Distance 6.5km Time 2 hours
Terrain clear paths, sometimes muddy
Map OS Explorer 410 Access regular ferry
service from Sconser to Churchton Bay:
no bus service on Raasay

Inverarish, the capital of Raasay, is an
attractive and very peaceful village. This
route explores its environs, starting from
the new ferry terminal and taking in the
harbour and coastline before returning
through the woods.

Begin the walk by turning left from the
ferry terminal to follow the track towards
the harbour. The stately pile visible from
the new ferry terminal is Raasay House;
Samuel Johnson and James Boswell
stayed here with the chief of Raasay John
MacLeod during their tour of the
Hebrides. In January 2009, just as a £4
million restoration programme was being
completed, fire ripped through the
community-owned building leaving just a
shell and the ornate facade. It is hoped
rebuilding work will return Raasay House
to its former glory and business and
community use.

Follow the track around a grassy
mound which once housed a gun
emplacement; on each side of it are two
huge stone mermaids commissioned by
the MacLeods and well worth popping up
the bank to examine closely. The cost of
the mermaids helped to ruin the island
chiefs, resulting in its eventual sale. This
proved a disaster for the people of Raasay
as one of the new owners, George Rainy,
carried out clearances of villages such as
Hallaig and Screapadal to make way for
sheep farms.

From the pier, continue round the grassy
curve of the next bay which forms a
harbour for local boats. At the far end,
waymarker posts direct you to a beautiful
grassy path which leads on towards the
headland. When the path forks, keep to the
right. The route now curves back to the
right along the top of the headland and is
well marked. At the woodland do not cross
the stile but keep left, passing through a

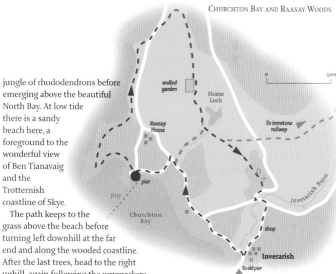

jungle of rhododendrons before emerging above the beautiful North Bay. At low tide there is a sandy beach here, a foreground to the wonderful view of Ben Tianavaig and the Trotternish coastline of Skye.

The path keeps to the grass above the beach before turning left downhill at the far end and along the wooded coastline. After the last trees, head to the right uphill, again following the waymarkers, and turning sharp right to reach a road. Turn left along the road for a short distance until a wide path goes off uphill into the pines on the right, signed for the Orchard Walk. Pass through a brief section of forestry to reach a giant stone wall; this once enclosed the orchards of Raasay House. Do not go through the gate; instead follow the wall right round the outside of the garden to the left. Beyond the orchard, a track is reached. Ignore the turning for Temptation Hill and turn left, passing alongside the pretty Loch a Mhuillin (Home Loch), forking left again at the end of the loch. The path now leads into the woods, soon reaching another junction; left leads to the Burma Road and can link with the Ironstone Mine walk (p86), but to continue this route keep

right. The path passes close by the ruins of Dun Borodale, an Iron Age stronghold known as a broch, almost smothered by the mossy trees. Emerge from the woods and pass the Manse, keeping straight on past the church to emerge on a road at a T-junction. Turn left at the junction and then right at the next one to descend through Inverarish, passing the shop and the terraced cottages. Turn right at the bottom of the hill and keep left to climb past the community hall before joining another road; keep left here past the church. Shortly beyond Borrodale House there is an old steading for Raasay House on the right; turn left here onto a tarmac lane that winds down, passing some cottages to Churchton Bay and the start of the walk.

◀ Raasay mermaid looking towards the Cuillin on Skye

The Ironstone Mine and the Burma Road

Distance 7km **Time** 2 hours 30
Terrain good paths, tracks and minor
roads **Map** OS Explorer 410 **Access** regular
ferry service from Sconser to Churchton
Bay: no bus service on Raasay

A slice of industrial history with views
of the Cuillin mountains as a backdrop,
this circular walk starts from Inverarish.
Peaceful Raasay was a hub of activity
when ironstone was mined here and,
during the First World War, German
prisoners of war built a railway and road
to serve it. Explore the remains of their
hard work on good paths with excellent
views over to Skye.

Approximately 200 people live on
Raasay, most in or near to Inverarish,
where the village shop also operates as a
post office and internet café. Just below
the shop, off the road, there is a parking
and picnic area. Alternatively, the village is
a short walk from the new ferry terminal
at Churchton Bay. From the shop,
walk down the double row of
terraced houses to the road

junction at the bottom and continue
straight ahead, following the road around
the coast to the left.

Just before the road reaches the
pier at Suisnish, look out for a signed
path heading uphill to the right. This path
follows the line of the steep ironstone
railway, where steam-powered, cable-driven
wagons used to bring the ore down from
the quarry to the jetty. On a clear day, as
you pass between derelict mine buildings
and continue to gain height, the
mountains across the water on Skye
become ever more spectacular. After the
initial climb, the route levels off and the
flat top of Raasay's long-extinct volcano,
Dun Caan, comes into view. When
Johnson and Boswell visited during
their tour of the Hebrides in 1773, Boswell
was so overcome by the view from Dun
Caan that he reportedly danced a jig on
the summit.

Continue along the line of the railway,
dipping into a cutting and up the other
side where an old bridge is missing.
Beyond this, enter the forestry

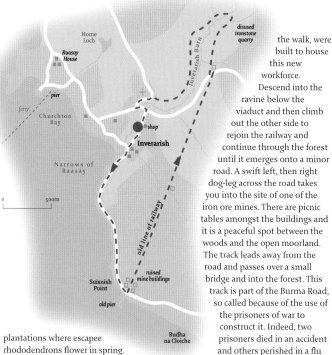

the walk, were built to house this new workforce.

Descend into the ravine below the viaduct and then climb out the other side to rejoin the railway and continue through the forest until it emerges onto a minor road. A swift left, then right dog-leg across the road takes you into the site of one of the iron ore mines. There are picnic tables amongst the buildings and it is a peaceful spot between the woods and the open moorland. The track leads away from the road and passes over a small bridge and into the forest. This track is part of the Burma Road, so called because of the use of the prisoners of war to construct it. Indeed, two prisoners died in an accident and others perished in a flu epidemic. After about 500m, the track reaches the site of the second mine. Here, a path leaves to the right, below a waterfall, for Dun Caan; stay on the main track as it curves to the left and heads downhill. Follow it through the woods, resisting the signed path for Temptation Hill. When the path reaches a road, turn left and then left again to walk through the village of Inverarish.

plantations where escapee rhododendrons flower in spring. After a short while, the ground dips away and the vast pillars of the now derelict viaduct loom up ahead. It is this structure that brings home the scale of this engineering project. The two ironstone mines only operated between 1913 and 1918, the workforce including men from Lanarkshire, Belgium and Italy as well as the German prisoners of war. The cottages at Inverarish, which will be passed later in

◄ The start of the railway incline at East Suisnish

Hallaig

Distance 6km **Time** 2 hours **Terrain** good path to the first ruin, then muddy **Map** OS Explorer 409 **Access** regular ferry service from Sconser to Churchton Bay: no bus service on Raasay

This walk follows an ancient path to the now deserted village of Hallaig. Made famous by the celebrated Gaelic poet Sorley MacLean, the ruined houses, set amidst a green, fertile sward, provide a haunting spot to ponder the lives of those who once lived here.

From the public road end at North Fearns, walk past the last house and follow a road which quickly becomes a path and is signed for Hallaig. The path is well-built and climbs gently uphill with superb views out towards the Crowlin Isles and the Applecross peninsula beyond. This is also a good spot to watch for schools of dolphins and porpoises which regularly pass through the Inner Sound. After the path turns a corner and nears the burn and woods, a memorial cairn is reached. A brass plaque is engraved with the words of Sorley MacLean's poem. Although the original poem was Gaelic, the version in English was translated by MacLean himself and even in this form it provides a moving testament to the love of this place by the people who lived there and the heartbreak and tragedy that their forced eviction brought. More recently Seamus Heaney wrote his own translation of the poem to commemorate the 150th anniversary of the Clearances here.

Continue on the path, passing the remains of a house to enter a birchwood (featured in the poem); the path from here on is boggy, and some may prefer to end the walk here. Go through the wood and cross the field beyond to reach a second section of birchwood. When the path runs downhill alongside a burn, cross it and ascend the steep muddy path on the far bank. When this emerges from the trees, leave it and follow the drystone wall uphill to reach the remains of the houses of Hallaig. The walls were built using stones from the houses after the village was cleared in 1854. In a period of just two years, 12 Raasay townships with a total of 94 families had been forced from their homes. The old cottages are spread out from here across the hillside towards Dun Caan.

The easiest way back to North Fearns is the same way. However, it is also possible for more experienced walkers to make a longer circuit by following an indistinct path from the point where the burn meets the Hallaig path, near the ruined house in the first birchwood, and to head directly uphill next to the burn. Once clear of the woods, this path follows a natural dyke to the west of Beinn na Leac, crossing boggy ground at times, to emerge on the road between Inverarish and North Fearns at a point where

there is a picnic table. If taking this route, you then turn left and follow the road downhill to return to the start at North Fearns.

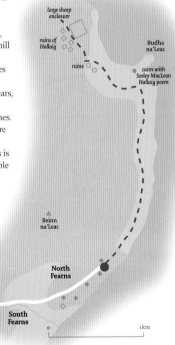

◀ *Looking towards Skye from North Fearns*

Screapadal and Brochel Castle

Distance 5.5km Time 2 hours
Terrain track and path, sometimes wet
Map OS Explorer 409 Access regular ferry
service from Sconser to Churchton Bay:
no bus service on Raasay

**An easy walk to the peaceful and
atmospheric ruins of the cleared township
of Screapadal. Here you can wander among
the stone remains of the blackhouses and
look out across the water to the mountains
of Applecross. The return route gives a
great view over the ruins of Brochel Castle,
once an impregnable fortress controlling
the waterway between Raasay and
the mainland.**

Heading north on the road to Arnish,
there is a small lay-by on the left just
before the dip down to Brochel. On the
opposite side of the road, a wooden sign
marks the start of the route to Screapadal.
Follow the track through a farm gate and
head downhill through recently cleared
forestry. The remains of a stone-built
house are passed on the right as you
zigzag down a steep section to the coast.

The track levels out and turns to the
right. Keep straight on, ignoring a turning
to the left which leads down to the pebbly
shore and a small jetty. When you reach
the end of the track, take a faint path
uphill beside a marker post. Follow some
rough cut stone steps down into a ravine
and cross a bridge over the small burn.
Rejoin the track up the bank and on
across the hillside.

Ahead, the green grass that was the site
of Screapadal comes into view. Screapadal

was cleared by the notorious Raasay landlord George Rainy. He built a wall blocking the islanders onto the barren north end of the island whilst keeping his stock on the better southern grazings.

Carry on along the track as it narrows and goes through a metal gate, passes below the houses of North Screapadal and crosses a burn on stepping stones before continuing on the other side. The best way to explore the ruins is to continue until you have just passed the ruins of South Screapadal up on the hill. As the gradient eases, climb up to the right to visit the ruins. From here, there is a good view of the houses of North Screapadal on the opposite hillside.

The easiest way back down from the houses is to head towards the section of path immediately above the wooden shed. Then retrace your steps back along the path and track. As the track starts to climb uphill, look out for a faint path on the right near the first corner. Follow this amongst the tree stumps and climb around the small headland. This part of the path is not waymarked and can be indistinct and boggy in places. Keep with it as it heads inland slightly and then down to a gate that emerges onto the road.

From here, you can turn right down the road for 100 metres to get a better view of Brochel Castle. Built in the late 15th or early 16th century by Raasay's first

MacLeod chief, Calum, the castle is situated on a volcanic plug and provided a strategic stronghold to control (and plunder) shipping on the Sound. Today much of the masonry is in decay, but the full structure would have had four high towers and presented an impregnable wall towards the sea. Turn back and return up the road to the parking area and the start of the walk.

◀ Brochel Castle

Inver Bay and the Sound of Raasay

Distance **3km** Time **1 hour 30**
Terrain **small but clear path**
Map **OS Explorer 410** Access **regular ferry service from Sconser to Churchton Bay: no bus service on Raasay**

This walk follows an old path by a burn and a rocky gorge to visit a lonely pebble beach. It has a fantastic outlook over the Sound of Raasay to the mountains of Skye and is the perfect place to sit and watch for sea eagles or wait patiently for a sighting of the elusive otter.

Approximately halfway along the road to the north end of Raasay, there is a parking area on the left where the road dips to cross a burn. A wooden signpost points the way to Inver, or in Gaelic, an t'Inbhir, meaning the mouth of the burn.

Go through the gate and pass the stone remains of the settlement of Brae. Walk downhill towards a farm gate but do not go through it; instead bear left through a smaller gate and a wooded glen. The path drops down the left side of this little

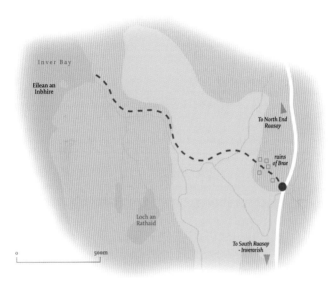

Inver Bay

Eilean an
Inbhire

To North End
Raasay

ruins
of Brae

Loch an
Rathaid

To South Raasay
- Inverarish

0   500m

birch-clad valley, and at its foot crosses a burn as it flows through a small rocky gorge with several pretty waterfalls.

Soon the path bears right and heads slightly uphill away from the water before sloping down through a more open area of heather and scattered trees. Further on, it runs alongside the burn once more, ending where it issues into the sea at a pebbly bay. This is Bagh an Inbhire, a fine spot for a picnic with its verdant grass.

Most of the bay can only be reached by paddling across the water, which can be impossible after wet weather, but this isn't really essential to enjoy the walk. The bay is a great place for wildlife spotting. Britain's largest bird – the white-tailed sea eagle – can frequently be seen here. Hunted to extinction in Victorian times, these magnificent birds were successfully reintroduced to the Isle of Rum in the 1980s and now have a viable population, mostly over Skye and Mull. Retrace your steps to the start.

◀ On the path to Inver Bay

Calum's Road, Torran and Fladday

Distance 5.5km **Time** 2 hours
Terrain good paths, sometimes wet
underfoot **Map** OS Explorer 409
Access regular ferry service from Sconser
to Churchton Bay: no bus service on Raasay

A chance to get away from it all by
following Calum's Road – the result of one
man's heroic struggle – to the north end of
Raasay. From here, a circular walk explores
rocky slopes and wooded dells to the tidal
crossing to the island of Fladday.

Drive up the road to the north end of
Raasay. One sign in Inverarish reads
'To the North Pole' and it does feel a bit
like that after a few miles of twisting road
through the barren part of the island.
Around 8km from Inverarish, shortly after
passing Brochel Castle, there is a

memorial cairn on the right-hand side.
This commemorates the work of one man
to extend the road for the next 3km to his
home village of Arnish. Exasperated with
the refusal by the local authority to
upgrade the footpath, and facing the
continuing depopulation of the area,
Calum set to work with a wheelbarrow
and pick-axe and almost single handedly
built the road to motorable standard.
When he finished in the mid 1970s, after
ten years of toil, he was the only man left
in north Raasay. His efforts have since
allowed a new generation of people to
return to Arnish and the north end, both
as crofters and holiday home owners.
The personal story and the history of
Raasay is set out in Roger Hutchinson's
bestselling book *Calum's Road*.

From the parking area at Arnish, follow the signed path left downhill, dodging the free-range pigs if they are about. The path winds through birchwoods before emerging to an excellent view of the Storr across the water. A short paved section leads to the old schoolhouse which is now a holiday home. Follow the path around the back of the building and then in front of a further building, signed for Fladday.

After passing another house, the path aims for a dip in the hills ahead and then crosses a steep rocky hillside on a stone-built raised terrace. As the path heads downhill, the island of Fladday comes into view. Once a thriving crofting community, the island now has three inhabitable houses and can be reached over seaweed-covered rocks at low tide.

Before you reach the shore, look out for a path on the right which climbs steeply at first and then levels off with great views back over Fladday to Skye. The next section can be wet underfoot, but it soon reaches drier ground. At the next junction turn right; the route to the left leads to the very north end of the island, a beautiful but very rough walk. Although the name Raasay means Island of the Roe Deer, red deer now populate the north end of the island. Follow the path all the way back to Arnish, passing a rocky cliff and crossing a stile before descending through a birchwood to

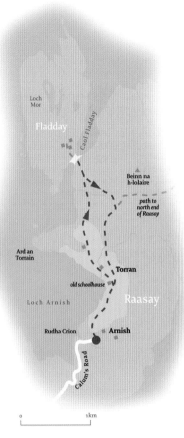

emerge behind the old schoolhouse. Turn left onto the outward path and follow it back to the parking area at the end of Calum's Road.

◄ On the road to Arnish

Index

An Aird	48
An Corran	16
Ardnish	60
Armadale	78
Arnish	94
Bearreraig Bay	8
Bioda Buidhe	18
Boreraig	68
Braes, The	46, 48
Broadford	56, 58, 60
Brochel Castle	90
Brothers' Point	12
Burma Road	86
Caisteal Maol	70
Calum's Road	94
Carbost	50
Churchton Bay	84
Claigan	34
Coille Iosal	46
Coire Lagan	54
Cuidrach	26
Cuillin	54, 64
Culnacnoc	12
Duirinish	36
Dun Ringill	62
Dun Scaith Castle	76
Duntulm	22
Dunvegan	36
Eas Mor	54
Elgol	64, 66
Fairy Pools	52
Fladday	94
Flodigarry	20
Glen Brittle	52, 54
Glendale	38
Hallaig	88
Hugh's Castle	26
Hunish	22
Inver Bay	92
Inverarish	84, 86
Kilmarie	62
Kilt Rock	6, 12
Kinloch Forest	74
Kirkibost	62
Kyleakin	70
Kylerhea	72
Lampay	34
Lealt	14
Leitir Fura	74
Loch Bracadale	40
Loch Coruisk	64
Loch Cuithir	14
Loch Snizort	26
Neist	38
North Fearns	88
Old Man of Storr	8, 10
Oronsay	40
Point of Sleat	80
Portree	42, 44, 46
Prince Charlie's Cave	66
Quiraing	20
Raasay	82, 84, 86, 88, 90, 92, 94
Score Horan	32
Scorrybreac	44
Screapadal	90
Skye Bridge	70
Sleat	56, 74, 76, 78, 80
Staffin	16, 18
Suisnish	68
Talisker Bay	50
Tokavaig	76
Torrin	68
Trotternish	6, 10, 12, 14, 16, 18, 20, 24, 26
Ullinish	40
Waternish	28, 30, 32